Anywhere But Here: Confessions of A Pisces Moon

B D SALERNO

Published by B D SALERNO, 2024.

While every precaution has been taken in the preparation of this book, the publisher assumes no responsibility for errors or omissions, or for damages resulting from the use of the information contained herein.

ANYWHERE BUT HERE: CONFESSIONS OF A PISCES MOON

First edition. January 21, 2024.

Copyright © 2024 B D SALERNO.

ISBN: 979-8988478553

Written by B D SALERNO.

Table of Contents

Anywhere But Here: Confessions of A Pisces Moon 1

INTRODUCTION 3

CHAPTER ONE | "I WANNA GO HOME" 5

CHAPTER TWO | PSYCHED OUT 15

CHAPTER THREE | CIAO, ITALIA 17

CHAPTER FOUR | FOLIES À DEUX 19

CHAPTER FIVE | THE SUMMER OF SEX 23

CHAPTER SIX | THE CITY OF LIGHT AND DARKNESS 29

CHAPTER SEVEN | ARRIVEDERCI, ITALIA 41

CHAPTER EIGHT | FROM FACTORY TO PHD 47

CHAPTER NINE | NEPTUNE'S LENS 51

CHAPTER TEN | PREDICTIVE PARANOIA 55

CHAPTER ELEVEN | EDGAR AND THE BEACH 61

CHAPTER TWELVE | NEW YORK MINUTES 69

CHAPTER THIRTEEN | COLLISION COURSE 73

CHAPTER FOURTEEN | THE HOUSE OF SICKNESS 77

CHAPTER FIFTEEN 99

CONTACT INFORMATION 111

The following is an autobiographical true account of many odd and unusual events in my life and the planetary activities that accompanied those events.

Some names have been changed to protect the innocent and guilty alike.

INTRODUCTION

I am very happy, and very blessed, to be alive today. There were times in my life when my death seemed predestined, but at a final critical moment, the script got rewritten.

I've led an unusual life for an introverted nerd. Unusual, and sometimes, catastrophic. Strange things have happened that in strange ways always made sense in the end. I didn't have a handle on this process until I came to learn the marvelous art and science of astrology.

I hope that my experiences will inspire others to learn more about astrology. But this not a book about astrology. It's really about my own personal struggles to find my place in the cosmos, and how divine intervention made its presence known at times.

Brief explanations of planetary activities have been added to explain critical situations, but you don't have to be an astrologer to appreciate this memoir. If you are or have ever been an outsider, gay, a baby boomer, a socially anxious nerd, seriously ill, involved in a fatality, lost without a compass, or a Sun/Moon/Rising in Pisces, hopefully this book will have something of value for you.

B.D. Salerno

April 7, 2025

CHAPTER ONE
"I WANNA GO HOME"

I entered this world on a crisp autumn day in October 1950 in the small blue-collar town of Rahway, NJ. Anxious fathers were not allowed in the delivery room in those days, so Loreto Salerno parked himself at a football field just up the street from the hospital and nervously watched the Saturday afternoon game. The Rahway High School football team, a perennial loser, was playing a tough local rival.

Just as I was making my worldly debut, the Rahway team pulled off an improbable upset against all odds - a truly Uranian moment. Loreto had no idea that his new baby daughter Barbara, born with Aquarius rising and her Pisces Moon in trine to Uranus in Cancer, would time and again also defeat the odds in seemingly improbable ways.

My first potentially traumatic incident occurred at the age of three, and it involved my father. He was working on the roof of our two-story duplex house with my Uncle John while I played alone in the backyard. I had admired how well Dad scaled the ladder going all the way up to the second story. Brash little tomboy that I was, I thought, "I can do that too!"

So up I went, one leg crossing a one rung at a time, until I had gleefully made it to the top of the ladder – well, almost. It was winter, and I was dressed in a heavy snowsuit. When I reached the top of the ladder my thickly padded leg couldn't reach up over the ladder frame and I got stuck right there at the top. The ladder began to sway.

At that moment my father, who had been preoccupied with his carpentry, spun around and saw me at the edge of the roof, struggling to swing my little leg up over the frame. Oh, the look of sheer terror and shock that registered on his face! It was priceless. I laugh about it now, but things could have gone disastrously bad for me.

He raced over, yanked me off the ladder and thrust me into a second story bedroom window. My Aunt Mary, who was in the bedroom, roughly pulled me through the window and spanked me on the spot. I was furious that my exciting ladder-climbing adventure had ended with such an indignity.

I was much too young to realize how lucky I was. I had escaped severe injury, disability, perhaps death, but good fortune prevailed, probably because of my lucky Jupiter rising. It was not the last time that I was spared a horrible fate, or the last time such a divine intervention would occur.

My precious Pisces Moon is intercepted in my first house. While it was often difficult for me to access my emotions I fell right in step with other Piscean interests at a very early age. Many of my relatives vacationed every summer at the Jersey shore, and I would accompany them, spending delightful months of swimming, fishing, and playing ball on the beach.

I quickly learned to swim, ride the waves, and surfboard with the best of them. I would play in the ocean until my skin shriveled like a prune. Anxious relatives often had to pull me out before I disappeared beneath the waves – an idea that held magical appeal for my Neptunian nature.

I also took to fishing – all kinds – trawling from my cousin's motorboat, fishing from a pier or jetty, or fishing in a fresh water pond. I rarely caught anything, but the biggest catch I ever got was the one that ended my fishing career forever. And it ended on a good note.

We lived near a park on the Rahway River, where I would spend lazy Saturday mornings fishing along its banks. The calmness and joy of spending a morning alone in nature more than made up for the lack of a catch. But then one came along, finally! A huge gold carp suddenly jerked my pole out of my hand and I had to scramble to reel him in. A fish at last, and a rare beauty too!

Fish in bucket, I raced home to show my parents the one and only catch of the day. Some time later I set up a small table with newspapers and knives in preparation for cleaning my prize, which my mother was going to cook for my dinner. But as I laid it out on the table the fish wiggled, its gills heaving in and out in a final desperate struggle to breathe. The fish had been in a bucket for hours but was miraculously still alive. In that moment something deep within me shifted.

"Dad, look! The poor thing is still breathing. He wants to live! We have to let him go." A Piscean Moon human sacrificing her dinner to rescue a fish, ruled by Pisces. I had no notions about astrology then, but it all felt so right.

My family, all animal lovers, respected my compassion. Dad quickly telephoned a friend whose private estate housed a nicely kept fish pond where the fish would not end up on someone's hook ever again. The fish splashed happily into its new home, having already forgotten the trauma of that afternoon. But I never did. Many years later, that same trauma of struggling mightily to breathe would pay an unwelcome visit.

Besides fishing I embraced all other things Piscean – the paranormal, ESP [Extra-Sensory Perception], the magical and the mysterious. My Sagittarian Mars gave me a love of sports, and I always rooted for the underdog.

With Mars square my Pisces Moon I was also drawn to music. My sister and I had piano lessons as a young child and I discovered that I could play melodies by ear. At the age of thirteen I picked up the guitar and taught myself to play folk music, following musicians like Joan Baez, Buffy Sainte-Marie and Bob Dylan with a passion.

Politically I was the typical liberal idealist of the Sixties, championing the cause of every lovable loser under the Sun. I had been taught the gift of giving second chances, even when the first one was ill earned. I was drawn to the illusory side of things, which often played itself out in some questionable choices of friends and other relationships. But it's the Pisces Moon way to behold beauty in a pile of steaming trash, even when there is nothing wrong with the eyes of the beholder.

Most Pisceans do not march to the beat of a different drum; they sway to the rhythm of offbeat celestial harmonies. A recurring desire of mine was to simply disappear into a background and remain undetected. Often in public I retreated into my wallflower persona, pretending to be invisible.

This desire for invisibility repeated itself time and again, especially when under emotional stress. It was difficult to weather tense confrontations, which in my home were plentiful, loud, and frequent. I would more easily fold like a cheap tent than square off against a tough adversary like my mother. The Piscean need for escape from adversity gave birth to one of my better skills: writing.

To offset the stress of frequent emotional turmoil I often retreated to my bedroom with pencil and paper in hand, where I would sit and write for hours on end. About anything, about anyone, about being anywhere, anywhere but here.

I took to writing from the moment I learned to form letters and numbers, and I wrote whatever came to mind – poems, songs, stories, even plays. Writing plays was especially gratifying. In plays people were having dialogue, they were communicating with each other - something that did not take place in a very rational manner within the four walls of our small two-bedroom house.

ANYWHERE BUT HERE: CONFESSIONS OF A PISCES MOON

I was born of a Sagittarian father and a Virgo mother – yeah, I know, they form a square to each other, and that is exactly what happened at home, my mom squaring off and berating my dad. Although they loved each other their personalities just clashed. My father was far too easygoing for my critical and perfectionist mother, who was damn near impossible to please. Both of them held very high standards for my sister and I, and seeking their approval seemed a fruitless exercise. Nothing was ever quite good enough, and the sting of a Virgo perfectionist's criticism can leave deep scars on a sensitive Pisces Moon child.

Yet I admired them both immensely. They had grown up through extreme deprivation during the Great Depression of the 1930s and had to go to work early in life to help support their families. My father, a rare high school graduate in his day, longed to attend college and law school, but then came his father's bankruptcy, early death, and World War II, where he spent three years in the Air Force.

His dreams denied, he ended up in sales, a pressure-packed position that drained his time and energy. Although he taught us to devote ourselves to doing something we love, he was never able to achieve that, and for most of my life neither was I.

My Virgo mom was a very kind, likable person, but for some odd reason she was very hard on her family. Growing up I feared her disapproval and criticism. But I admired her enormously, and still do. She was the classic Supermom of the Fifties – house spotless, clothing always cleaned and pressed, lunch boxes packed and ready to go, appointments all kept on time, budgets managed to the penny. There was nothing she wasn't capable of doing, and doing well. But she had a volatile personality: Her Leo Mercury squared her Scorpio Mars, and she could cut you to the quick with an abusive remark, leaving deep psychic scars.

My mother had grown up during the 1920s on the wrong side of the tracks, in a poor family of ten children who shared a cramped three-room house with an outhouse in the back yard. She knew all about hardship and sacrifice, having been forced to quit school at the age of 12 to work at demanding menial jobs that paid very little. Her own early life was marred by an abusive mother, overwhelming responsibilities, and domestic violence.

In spite of these shortcomings my mother was an exceptional person. She was adaptable and strong-willed, as was my father, and when she set her mind to something she achieved it.

At the age of 45 my father taught her to play golf, and four years later she became the club champion, winning eleven championships in the following years and numerous tournaments and prizes around the tri-state area. Helen Salerno's name was often in the local paper. She played golf until the age of 87 and she could have kept on going even then.

It was Mom's emotional instability that contributed to my writing skills; her outbursts drove me into the seclusion of my bedroom, pencil and pad in hand, where words provided the escape hatch from my unhappy reality. Life is funny that way.

And my birth chart also features a blessed mutual reception between seventh house Saturn in Virgo and eighth house Mercury in Libra: Writing helped heal me and transform me. Besides Mom, it was the Universe's way of providing a creative outlet for some of the emotional challenges that came my way.

Another great love also came very early in life, as soon as I could walk. Whenever my parents brought me outside at night I would gaze in awe at the night sky. The stars were so sparkling and inviting and I wanted

ANYWHERE BUT HERE: CONFESSIONS OF A PISCES MOON

to visit them and play with them. The old Disney song, "Would you like to swing on a star," suited me perfectly.

The night sky always blanketed me with a sense of peace and comfort that I never experienced at home, and it became my distant refuge. On one star-gazing evening out my bedroom window I felt a small cry bubbling up from within. I heard myself whimper, "I wanna go home."

Home was not the turbulent family house on Whittier Street; home was light years away, and I was human years away from realizing its blessings. But that was where my father stepped in. He had noticed my fascination with the stars and it resonated deeply with him; he had been a flight navigator in the Army Air Force during World War II. His job was to navigate the night sky during secret flight missions over the Pacific.

As flight navigator it was incumbent upon him to calculate the right coordinates using the night stars, lists of numbers, and pages of dizzying coordinates. He recounted to me many times how terrifying it was to be responsible for the lives of his flight crew. They had no computers for this; Dad had to do all the manual calculations with a stubby little pencil on lined graph paper. Any mistake could expose his B29 bomber and the flight crew to catastrophe, but he was bound and determined not to let that happen.

My father, a jovial Sun-Venus Sagittarian with a pleasant Libra Moon, made the most of his Capricorn Mars. His work ethic was impeccable - persistent and determined beyond all stubbornness. Thanks to that he and his flight crew flew 21 successful secret missions over Japanese territories. He survived the war and I got the chance to carry on his legacy of guidance by the stars.

When I was nine years old Dad bought me a telescope and we would retreat to the back yard for nightly sky viewings. No matter how raw the bitter New Jersey winters, I would bundle up and go outside at midnight, when viewing of the winter sky was best. It couldn't be too cold for me; I was in my element and loved every minute of it.

Dad taught me how to locate Polaris, the north star, several different ways: By drawing a line from the central point of the 'W' in the constellation Cassiopeia, from the edge of the Big Dipper, from the belt of Orion. From Sirius I would find the northward sweeping ridge of the fixed stars Procyon, Pollux, Castor, Menkalinen, Capella. There were so many mystical stars: Betelguese in the shoulder of Orion, Rigel at his feet, Sirius the Dog Star, Alcyone in the nose of Taurus the Bull. Canis Major and Minor, a large and a small dog, remain forever close by Orion's side as his hunting companions.

It fascinated me that the three finely aligned stars in the belt of Orion were actually thousands of light years apart from each other, and that their light had been transmitted from the stars many thousands of years before it even reached me. I was glimpsing eternity at a glance. I had no idea then that many of these fixed stars would surface decades later in my forensic astrology research, when I too, like my father before me, would calculate their celestial positions.

Astronomy was not my only fascination as a child. I remained intensely drawn to things outside the normal realm of perception, things to which Pisces is well attuned. I had an uncanny sense of psychic foreboding at times, like I did one night when I was thirteen years old. The Pisces Moon is highly intuitive, subject to receiving impressions in inexplicable ways. Sometimes we also receive foreboding signs and symbols of events just before they happen.

It was an ordinary Thursday evening, only memorable because of the catastrophic events that followed. I was in bed reading a Cliff Notes style paperback about psychology, my favorite subject, when things got weird.

ANYWHERE BUT HERE: CONFESSIONS OF A PISCES MOON

One chapter described projection – the displacement of one's feelings onto others. It gave examples of how people often project negative feelings about their parents onto authority figures – a man hates his boss because his father was cruel, another steals from a bank because his family had no money, and so on.

The text gave another example, a disturbing one – that a man who harbors ill will against his father may, under certain conditions, want to assassinate the President of a country.

An assassination? What a horrible thought! John F. Kennedy, the current President, was an inspiration to us young people. I couldn't wrap my head around the idea of someone shooting him; it would paralyze the entire country. Psychology sure was scary at times.

The next day was a Friday. I usually liked Fridays but this day brought a twinge of apprehension. I kept asking my mother, was it a holiday? Something just felt off.

My mom had laid out a colorful sweater and skirt outfit for me to wear to school, but for some odd reason I insisted on wearing black – black knee socks, black shoes, a black skirt, a white blouse with a black vest over it, and a black scarf.

I didn't have any idea why I was feeling this way, but when I met my friend Sue at school that morning she remarked, "Why are you all dressed in black, you going to a funeral or something?" to which I could only reply, "No, it just feels like some kind of sad holiday."

The day was Friday, November 22, 1963. Five hours later President Kennedy was shot and killed in front of the Texas School Book Depository in Dallas, Texas. My friend Sue could not get over it. "I can't believe you wore black today! What the heck?" I had no answer for her. That foreshadowing, or whatever it was, had me spooked for days afterward. I still get a surreal feeling when I think of it.

What were the heavens up to then? Transiting Jupiter in Aries was exactly square my natal fifth house Uranus in Cancer; transiting Sun in ninth house Scorpio was squaring my natal Jupiter on my Aquarius Ascendant; transiting Saturn in Aquarius was exactly trine my natal Neptune in Libra from the twelfth to the eighth houses – death and subterfuge – while Moon was hiding out in the twelfth at that same time.

Lilith, the evil witch, sat perched at my Midheaven in Sagittarius, symbolizing the abject evil about to be cast upon the collective consciousness of the country. That wasn't all, either – Venus and Mars were also slow dancing together in Sagittarius, conjoining my natal tenth house Mars.

So much Sagittarius! Kennedy's foreign policies, especially his opposition to the war in Vietnam, threatened the status quo of certain military and government figures, resulting in a coup that destabilized the country, setting it up for a whole new regime. Things would never be quite the same again. Nor would I.

CHAPTER TWO
PSYCHED OUT

As time flew forward I maintained an avid interest in all things occult and supernatural. My busy eighth house, packed with Neptune, Mercury, Venus, and the Sun in that order, promised me a lifetime of delving into the depths of these subjects.

My shadowy experience with the JFK assassination had convinced me to study psychology at Rutgers University in the women's college, then known as Douglass College. Psychology studies would feed my ravenous eighth house need to probe human behavior and investigate the human mind. So I registered as a psychology major and immediately made my first classic blunder.

With Aquarius rising I've always been determined to do things my own way, not always the best way. I did not take the typical Psychology 101 lecture class, but instead launched right into the meat and potatoes of the curriculum. I had enjoyed laboratory work in my high school science classes and signed up right away for a statistics course that required demanding laboratory experiments and extremely technical write-ups. The department put a heavy emphasis on clinical psychology, requiring extremely exacting courses in statistics and research design, not to mention, advanced mathematics, not my strong suit.

As a naïve freshman I was completely outmatched by the mental demands placed upon me, and I wasn't faring well with the math or the statistical analysis. I also did not relish spending my early Saturday mornings rewarding a cageful of white lab rats with chocolate milk as a reward for learning how to push a button on a dial.

When the Dean of the Psychology Department called me into her office I knew it wasn't a good sign.

"Miss Salerno, is there anything else you can major in? You are about to flunk out of this class." Psyched-out is the word for how I felt at the moment. I took the hint, bailed out of Psych, and signed up to major in languages. With an Aquarian Jupiter rising on my Ascendant I was interested in all things foreign. Jupiter gave a helpful trine to my eighth house Sun, Venus, and Mercury, so languages came easily to me.

I had always wanted to study Russian; my maternal ancestors were from Ukraine and the Cyrillic alphabet held strong fascination for me. But the classes for Russian 101 were always full during those cold war years when Russian interpreters were in demand. I didn't know it then, but this interest in translating and interpreting signs and symbols would serve me very well in future years in an altogether unexpected way.

CHAPTER THREE
CIAO, ITALIA

After the debacle with the Psych Department I chose to major in Italian and English. I had taken four years of Latin studies in high school and Italian was based on Latin, which proved helpful. In Italian class we were encouraged to correspond with pen pals in Italy. I became pen pals with a girl in the Lombardy region of northern Italy and we exchanged frequent letters.

The influence of foreigners and foreign countries rings loud in the career sector of my chart. Sagittarius lies at the Midheaven, with Mars there in the Virgo degree. Its ruler, Jupiter in Aquarius, embraces my Ascendant; I have always had many friends from foreign countries.

Years later, as a paralegal, I corresponded with corporate clients and attorneys in practically every country in the world. Jupiter, ruling my Midheaven, is in the Gemini degree, indicating that correspondence was also a mainstay of my profession. Corresponding with a foreign pen pal allowed me to delve right into the language and culture, not to mention, have someone to visit in Italy.

Her name was Emma. We became close friends through our correspondence, and she invited me to visit her in the summer of 1970. I didn't dare ask my parents to fund the trip; my father was already in debt with college loans. So I worked part-time during the school year and part of the summer and managed to save up just enough money for the trip. By the first week of August I was bound for Milan via Alitalia Airlines.

Transiting Neptune was squaring my Jupiter for a long distance dream voyage, and transiting Jupiter was conjunct my Sun, bolstering my enthusiasm for the distant voyage while providing protection for the journey. Neptune was also transiting my ninth house of long-distance journeys, and would expose a new talent: taking good photographs.

I spent six weeks traveling and visiting with my pen pal's family, even locating my father's ancestors in a small village high in the mountains of the Abbruzzi province. It was the trip of a lifetime, fulfilling the dream offered by Neptune. I fell head over heels in love with the Italian landscape, the food, the language, its spectacular architecture and artistic achievements. And Emma and I had become fast friends. As soon as I left I felt a deep longing to return.

I made it my goal to return to Italy the following summer – this time, for the entire three months. I got a job at a convenience store where I worked 24 hours every weekend. With a full course load I rarely had a day off but I was all in, and the sacrifice would be worth it. Little did I know that my second trip would be nothing short of disastrous.

CHAPTER FOUR
FOLIES À DEUX

My junior year classes began the day after I returned from Italy, jet-lagged and disoriented. While moving into new dorm accommodations I started up a conversation with an attractive young French student, a freshman who had just arrived on campus. Her name was Gigi Bouchard. When I told Gigi I had just been to Italy she took an immediate interest, and we became fast friends.

Gigi was from Paris by way of New York; her father was an accountant there and her mother lived in the south of France. Her backstory, being an illegitimate child reared by a single French woman in the Paris slums, was both legendary and notorious. She had left home at the age of 13 to run with a motorcycle gang, somehow managing to survive until her father brought her to the States for her high school and college education.

Gigi was smart beyond her years, much more street smart than I, and extremely perceptive. As different as my life as a sheltered nerd had been, we met on the same intellectual level, and quickly became inseparable. We spent many nights sitting up late, talking and laughing over coffee and cigarettes.

We were always away from campus on the weekends: I worked at the convenience store near my parents' house while Gigi visited her boyfriend Rob at Temple University in Pennsylvania. Every Sunday night after we returned to campus we would get together and talk late into the night. No subject was off limits. In time I felt like I could tell her anything. In time she would tell me things too, and sometimes they were things I wasn't ready to hear.

Gigi was attractive, smart, and engaging, with deep green eyes, dirty blond hair, and a very fit, slender body. Unlike the rest of us, whose self-esteem was easily shaken, she exuded an aura of confidence and self-assurance well beyond her eighteen years. I had never known anyone quite like her.

Opposites attracted: Her smooth, confident demeanor somehow complemented my nerdy awkwardness, and we got along famously. They say that Librans are gifted with charm, but as a sheltered introvert I was hard pressed to find that attribute within myself, even with four Libran planets pitching in.

Nothing was typical about Gigi. She could sport a tattered t-shirt and a beat-up pair of jeans and still command a runway performance. I was totally enchanted by her, but I would not realize the extent of my feelings until it was uncomfortably, and irrevocably, too late. An intercepted Pisces Moon can have trouble accessing feelings, and it would take a jarring experience to dislodge what was brewing inside me. Sometimes even the Pisces Moon doesn't fully realize what lies hidden there beneath its dreamy surface.

When I told Gigi of my plans to spend the summer in Europe she jumped at the idea. "Hey, I'm going to visit my Mom in Toulouse for the summer. Let's go together! You can stay with me in France and then go on to Italy." It sounded perfect - too good to be true. My plans had never included anyone else, but that changed in a heartbeat. Little did I know what a colossal debacle lie waiting across the pond.

As spring semester drew to a close Gigi made travel arrangements for us both. I had managed to scrimp together exactly $1,000 from my weekend job. I needed only $200 for the discount student round trip charter flight to London, and the remaining $800 would have to get me through the rest of the summer. Back then the purchase power of the dollar was extremely strong in Europe, but I didn't care about the

ANYWHERE BUT HERE: CONFESSIONS OF A PISCES MOON

essentials – I would have slept on a park bench just to be back in Italy again.

Oh, to have been an astrologer, and foreseen what a dreadful, horrendous set of planetary aspects conspired to ruin that trip! The hits kept coming for three months straight, thanks to hyperactive Saturn, Uranus, Neptune and Pluto, a veritable rat pack of celestial scoundrels seriously intent on wrecking my plans.

To begin with, on the day of our departure transiting Saturn was precisely conjoining the mother of malevolent fixed stars, Algol, in my third house of travel. I was lucky just to have survived without some physical calamity (although I would come very close in the ensuing months). For the duration of the summer transiting Uranus in my eighth house was forming a square to its natal position in my fifth house. Anyone for sex, conventional or otherwise? A foreshadowing of some romantic complications maybe?

I was in for the shock of my life in that regard. Sex would become a main theme of the day, or should I say, the entire summer. Like the proverbial saying, water, water was everywhere, but not a drop to drink. At least not for me, anyway. Gigi, on the other hand, would be well hydrated for the duration while I continually thirsted for things well out of my reach. I would become a human drought in the midst of a deluge.

Last but not least, Pluto, which resides in my natal sixth house, had moved up to crush my seventh house Saturn, where it was annihilating the boundaries and structures I had built around relationships. And relentless Pluto would not let up.

Our first stop was in London for a few days, and then on to Paris by way of the ferry across the English Channel. I didn't know astrocartography then, but if I had, I would have cancelled out the entire trip and then some: My Pluto line draped itself across England, targeting London with deadly pinpoint accuracy. Pluto the annihilator, discovered during the development of the atomic bomb! Let the nuclear games begin.

CHAPTER FIVE
THE SUMMER OF SEX

Gigi and I headed off to Kennedy Airport on an early June day. This was the long-awaited day that I had slaved and saved for, but instead of excitement, I felt apprehension and dread, and I couldn't put my finger on why. Gigi would do that for me.

When we reached the terminal for the charter flight, a drab outbuilding on the dreary outskirts of JFK Airport, it was jam-packed with students – students bearing backpacks, guitars, duffel bags, long scruffy hair, fringed suede jackets, marijuana joints rolled up in bandanas, and scuffed boots - the complete unwashed look of the early Seventies.

While waiting to board the flight Gigi struck up a conversation with a shaggy-haired hippie-looking guy who was obviously interested in her. The two began flirting. As we lined up to board the plane we got separated, so I grabbed a seat near the front of the aircraft and waited for her to appear. Somehow, though, she had gotten ahead of me.

As I scanned the rear of the plane, there she was, already engaged in a heavy petting session with Hippie Guy. They were all over each other, right there in the coach seats, arms stroking and tongues locking. I did a double take, hoping against hope that it was maybe someone else, but there they were, going at each other like hungry lions tearing at prey. I was dumbstruck.

Had I known the chaos that lay ahead of me I would have jumped off the plane right then and there. But this was the trip I had painstakingly worked toward for the past ten months. I couldn't fathom just abandoning it. If I had only known the astrology for those summer months I would not only have gone home, I would have locked myself in a closet for the next three months. Funny how the trip would soon involve a different kind of closet, but later for that.

Gigi's behavior baffled me. We had talked endlessly about this trip with such anticipation but we didn't even sit together on that six-hour flight. Hippie Guy had somehow smuggled alcohol onto the plane and the two of them were happily numbing themselves. By mid-flight I could have used a large dose of anesthesia myself.

As the long flight finally touched down at Gatwick I convinced myself that Gigi was just letting loose, and I was being too much of a Debbie downer. After all, here we were with Europe at our feet, so let's make the most of it.

That steely resolve melted into a puddle about ten hours later. We had reserved a cheap room in a London boarding house, our first stop after arrival. To my annoyance, Hippie Guy tagged along; he had ignored my unfriendly sideways glances and invited himself to crash with us. My initial inklings of doom were about to overflow.

We went out to a pub that night with Hippie Guy still tagging along, irritating me no end. I dreaded returning to the room, where there were only two beds; God knew how that was going to work out, and soon I did too.

The lovebirds cozied up in one bed while I, tingling with apprehension, crawled into the other. It didn't take long. The sounds of a creaking rickety mattress accompanied by loud moans began to fill the air. Really, I thought, right in front of me? Is this really happening? Or am I lying in a coma somewhere? Did I hit my head and pass out? Or did the plane crash and I died and went straight to Hell?

"Hey Barb, you want to join in?" croaked a sultry voice from beneath the sheets of the bed where the two passionate lovers lay gyrating. How thoughtful of them! I couldn't believe it. "Uh, um, no thanks." I buried my head beneath a stack of pillows and tried to convince myself it was all a sick porno dream complete with sleazy sound effects.

By the time I awoke in the morning Hippie Guy had thankfully departed. My timid first-house Pisces Moon never liked direct confrontations, but my Aquarian Ascendant took over – I just had to say something. I had not seen anything remotely close to this side of Gigi and some words were in order.

"Why were you with that scruffy guy?" I challenged her. "He wasn't even your type!!"

Gigi replied in her usual cool nonplussed way, "Oh, I'm on vacation now. I just want to have fun." I don't think screwing a creepy guy right in front of your best friend was exactly what Cyndi Lauper had in mind when she sang her iconic hit song "Girls Just Wanna Have Fun," but there it was. Vacation - rhymes with abomination.

My poor Pisces Moon! I had no idea of the emotional battering she was about to take, and things were only just getting started. But I kept reminding myself that I was finally back in Europe and not to let things go awry so early. I remained at Gigi's side, suffering in silence.

Where did we end up the very next night? In a nightclub surrounded by hungry young men on the prowl, one of whom she promptly picked up and brought back to the room. This time outspoken Aquarius rising vetoed timid Pisces Moon once again. I was not about to suffer through another miserable sex session courtesy of Gigi and her latest *amour du jour*.

"Listen, guys, can't you go somewhere else?" Her companion offered to take us over to his flat. I declined, not so politely, but off went Gigi, beau in arm, for another night of fun and frolic in ye jolly olde London town.

I remember sitting up in a musty old armchair through that entire night, teary-eyed and freezing. It was rainy and cold there in early June and I had no change to put into the coin-operated heater. I sat awake pondering why Gigi had suddenly chosen to channel her inner nymphomaniac, devouring two guys in two days. The sheer craziness of her sudden shift in behavior was unnerving.

But there lay London at my feet, which was such a popular hot spot since the British music invasion of the Sixties. I had wanted to see it all – Westminster Square, Piccadilly, Kensington Gardens, Big Ben over the Thames – and we had only a few days to spend. We got to visit each of these legendary venues and happily got along quite well during those trips.

Most of all, I was determined to visit the "mod" hot spot of Carnaby Street, the seat of hip London fashion at the time. We made our way to the shops where Gigi purchased a dressy skin-tight long-sleeved blouse to augment her nightclub wardrobe.

Upon boarding an imposing red double-decker bus I was amused to note a sign over the entrance: Mind Your Head. The double entendre registered with me. I wish I could have taken that sign home as a souvenir. I really did need to mind my head, and not in the literal sense. I needed to get a handle on what was going on with Gigi, how it would impact my trip, and what, if anything, I could do to just roll with it – or roll away from it.

I pondered the issue intensively. I thought of all our talks about the types of people we were attracted to, and neither of her guys remotely fit the bill. I thought of her poverty-stricken childhood in Paris, when she had become a street urchin at the age of thirteen, running with a gang of kids, sleeping with men at fourteen, even having a lesbian affair with her school headmistress at the age of sixteen. Gigi was eighteen going on forty.

ANYWHERE BUT HERE: CONFESSIONS OF A PISCES MOON

I thought of poor steadfast Rob back home, to whom she had been faithful all throughout the school year – what on earth would he think now? Finally, I thought of Dr. Jekyll and Mr. Hyde, and settled on that for a quick and dirty explanation of Gigi's wild behavioral change. Vacation, indeed.

Naturally, the new, wild-spirited Gigi was great fun to hang out with, especially in clubs and bars. We would laugh and dance wildly to the music while she managed to inveigle free drinks from male customers who ogled, and approved of, her thigh-high skirts, skin-tight tops, and sexy flirtations.

She also had the outrageous habit of hopping from table to table at night's end and drinking the remnants of any glasses that had not yet been cleared away, regardless of their contents. While I found this immensely amusing, I never tried it myself.

Gigi and I reached an agreement - she would drop me off at the hotel before taking off with some dude, which was fine, until it wasn't. Something had begun to boil inside of me, and it smelled like Pluto slashing and burning his way across Saturn's stern structure in my seventh house of relationships. That transit would grind away, on and off, for the next three months like an atom smasher in a laboratory.

Pluto, and then Uranus, finally forced me to confront what was really bubbling up inside of me. It wasn't that her behavior was just so suddenly raunchy. Truth be told, I was jealous - insanely so. I wanted to be that guy in her bed. Oh Lord. Here came the wrath of Uranus rearranging my sexuality, and I was light years from being ready for that invasion.

And Pluto, never an energy to take lightly, packed such a heavy punch that summer. Of course it involved sexual excess, but not mine, darn it. Water, water, everywhere ...

And Uranus, with its out-of-left field craziness and unconventionality! Of course I had to get in touch with scary, previously unexplored feelings about my own sexuality that I has avoided dealing with for years. Since childhood I knew I was "different" that way, but for years I continued to sail down that deep dark river in Egypt until my leaky emotional Piscean barge began taking on water.

Prodded by Pluto, I had to confront deep-seated jealousies, sexual frustrations, and manipulations. Pluto knew no boundaries and could have cared less how much I wanted to apply the brakes to his visit. Of course I was consumed by toxic outbursts of jealousy, feelings of inadequacy, and easily damaged self-esteem. Those were the order of the day, and these astral giants were not about to let me off the hook just because I was finally on my long-awaited dream trip.

It felt so unfair for my naïve 20-year old psyche to endure such a barrage of torturous feelings while on the adventure of a lifetime, but there you have it. Gigi had, unknowingly or not, set the stage for the melodramatic debacle to unfold. And we hadn't even gotten to Paris yet. I was about to learn the true meaning of the phrase "Paris when it sizzles." Once there I would get burned yet again.

CHAPTER SIX
THE CITY OF LIGHT AND DARKNESS

The ferry ride from London to Paris briefly took my mind off my misery. Like the airport, it was packed with students on summer break, backpacking their way through the Continent. While on board I conversed with a few friendly travelers who helped to buoy my sinking feelings about the trip.

Gigi too had been meeting people, and going home with them after a wild night of partying. I grudgingly accepted her newfound nymphomania but stayed true to my conservative, reserved nature. On the outside, that is. Inwardly, my heart was inflamed with a passionate and consuming jealousy, while my mind grappled with what those intense feelings meant.

It wasn't cool to be gay in the Sixties, or for that matter, in the Seventies. Or at any other time in history up to that point. It was something that split apart families, that cost people their jobs, that got kids kicked out of their homes, their churches, their schools. It was something that both kids and adults even killed themselves over.

Like practically everyone in the Fifties, especially Roman Catholics, I had grown up indoctrinated by the most deranged inflammatory rhetoric about homosexuality. The words "faggot" and "lesbian" were equivalent to curse words that we weren't allowed to say. And the poor unfortunates to whom those labels were attached suffered untold emotional burdens.

I remember hearing old witches' tales about lesbians – how they would attack single women alone in an alleyway, in a bathroom - even in an elevator, of all ridiculous places. "The Lesbian Elevator Attacks" sounded like a perfect title for a future spoof story, and I tucked it away in my mental files. The anti-gay and lesbian propaganda was asinine and idiotic, but it was a fixture in people's prejudices and dominated social convention at that time.

Lesbians were ugly women who dressed like men, who smoked cigars and sported crew cuts, who were doomed to spinsterhood or to each other because they could never get a man. While I'm not especially feminine, the very smell of cigars makes me violently ill. I've had close friendships with both men and women, gay and straight alike. I do admit to a preference for tailored clothing, the type men wear, but it's really all about whom you love, not what you look like or what you wear.

It was liberating to finally acknowledge my gayness, but worrisome in regard to my family, my friends, and my career. It would have to be kept secret, deeply buried under cover, adding stress to my already awkward and painful social anxiety. As freewheeling and loose as the Sixties were, gay was still a very touchy subject. You had to be extra careful who you told and hope that word didn't travel very far.

I had had inklings of my gayness ever since childhood, but never met the issue head-on – it had to hit me with a sledgehammer. Now, on my once-upon-a-time trip of a lifetime, I was at a total loss as to how to handle it. There I was, in a strange country thousands of miles from family and friends, not very conversant in French, completely alone. Gigi, my best friend, was either not there in the flesh or emotionally unavailable. I was trying to process an enormous elephant in the room with no one to talk to or seek advice from, and it was threatening to crush me.

The truth of the matter was undeniable: I was madly in love with my best friend, and it was killing me to watch her run around with trashy guys, or with any guy, for that matter. It was a lonely and confusing time.

Gigi and I were managing to get along, but not for long. Upon our arrival in Paris she seemed fidgety, well out of character for her usually cool and collected demeanor. After deboarding the ferry we walked a few blocks and stopped at a sidewalk café, which felt odd, as we still had all our luggage with us.

"Where is our hotel? Shouldn't we check in and drop off these suitcases first?" I inquired. She shrugged. My gut started to churn. Why had I entrusted her with the hotel arrangements?

"I don't know yet," she said to my amazement. She began conversing with an older Senegalese man who had been sitting nearby, obviously taking her in. He had noticed our suitcases alongside our chairs, figured out our situation, and made his move.

They spoke briefly in French. Suddenly they both arose from the table. Gigi said with a frown, "Let's go, we're going to the room now." Uh-oh. What room? Five minutes ago she didn't know about a room. My nerves bristled with apprehension.

Suitcases in hand, we trudged over to a building on rue Recamier where there was a dormitory that housed foreign students, many of whom were from Senegal. We trudged up several flights of stairs to a dank, tiny room with a narrow cot pushed against one wall and a small sink sectioned off from the room by a dingy threadbare curtain. It looked nothing like a hotel room. As if on cue Gigi announced, "I'll be right back," and left the room with the man. Now what?

They returned not too long afterward, and then the man excused himself and left. Gigi had a disgusted look on her face, as if she had just sucked a bag of lemons - and who knows what else.

"Shit! That old dude probably hasn't fucked anybody in like twenty years," she grumbled.

I shot back, "Are you for real? Did you really just screw that guy?" The word "fuck" was still not bandied about as loosely as it is now; we had all been taught never to say it, but "screw," in all its meaning, was an even better choice. To screw – to twist a sharp metal bit deeply into a softer, more pliant surface until it took hold – I was getting to know the feeling well. And I also knew the answer to my question.

"Look, we had no place to go, and he offered us this room for a few days for free. I didn't know there were strings attached until it was too late, and I didn't want to make him mad." No way was the room really free, but I let Gigi slide on that one.

"You're crazy. What are we gonna do in this shithole of a room with that pervy guy hanging around?" I was beyond freaked. Gigi had no reply.

Shithole was the operative word; the toilets in the hallway consisted of a large fetid, stinking hole in the floor that you had to squat over in order to relieve yourself. Two narrow cement footrests on either side of the hole allowed you to steady yourself while doing so. I often felt nauseated while using the filthy facility, and I could never relieve myself and get the hell out of there fast enough.

We made do with the tiny room for a few more days, as we had already booked a small puddle-jumper flight from Orly Airport to Toulouse where Gigi's mother lived. I had to bide my time and wait.

Naturally, every night was spent at some Parisian waterhole where we danced like demons, drank, and met various people of all persuasions. Gigi was the talk of every bar we frequented, scoring us free food and drink in the magical, seductive way only she could muster.

ANYWHERE BUT HERE: CONFESSIONS OF A PISCES MOON

But there was one catch, unbelievably: The room did not belong to the older Senegalese guy after all. It belonged to a young friend of his who had no idea that his room had been offered as a crash pad to two teenaged female travelers.

Joseph was a tall, muscular Senegalese student with strikingly attractive coal-black features. When he arrived at his room to find two teenaged girls there he registered both confusion and joy. I was apprehensive beyond belief at how this new arrangement was going to fly.

Had I known the French language, known how to get around, or at least had some connections to a sane outside world things might have been different, but I didn't, so I stuck it out. I had already weathered some tough times, and I was still struggling with my fragile and frustrated sexuality. It was a recipe for how you would expect Uranus, Pluto and Saturn to turn out if you tossed them all into a blender with a side of Venus and turned it on high speed.

The first night in Joseph's room was eventful. He slept on the floor while Gigi and I snuggled together in the cot. Finally I was close to her again, close enough to smell her hair and cuddle, spooning my body against hers. I was beginning to enjoy this new arrangement, until with one sweep of his arm Joseph pulled her down onto the floor and they engaged in rough sex right then and there. I was infuriated and hurt beyond belief, but that was not the moment to act out. I just had to wait it out. But patience was in very short supply.

We buzzed our way through Paris, lounging around sidewalk cafes by day and hitting the clubs by night. Ironically, I too was drawing interest from men in the clubs, about the last thing I wanted. My reserved behavior was a stiff contrast to that of my wanton companion, who had forgotten how to say "no" in any language.

The club and sidewalk café scene quickly became tiresome, so I finally set out on a tour of the city alone, armed with only a map of the Paris Metro. Gigi was not interested in the museum circuit so I became my own tour guide, and happily discovered that I could navigate the Paris Metro with ease.

The most thrilling moment came when I was able to view the Mona Lisa, "La Gioconda," at the Louvre. For all its storied drawing power this iconic and timeless painting is small, measuring just 30 by 21 inches. Wow, I thought, the incredible allure of this painting had always made it seem larger than life, yet up close and personal it looked so diminutive. It was beginning to sink in that other things around me held the same false allure.

Slumming on my own gave me a sense of independence and release from Gigi and her antics. I grew comfortable traversing the rues and boulevards of Paris on my own – but not completely. Public transportation for a single teenaged female posed its own set of risks, as I would find out on one Metro ride.

While standing near the exit door a man sidled up close behind me, which was odd as that train car was empty. He began to press his pasta-padded gut, and parts beneath it, into my backside. Gusts of his heavy garlic-laced breath wafted up into my nostrils. Oh this is too much, I thought: Gigi, my one heart's desire, remained aloof and disinterested, while men were aplenty, willing and able. Sheer anger laced with frustration got the better of me – the one and only that I yearned for was unavailable, yet here was some poor slob poking me in the rear on a train. Enough was enough! In a flash of a moment my inner trigger was primed for retaliation.

I raised my elbow and brought it down as hard as possible into Mr. Pasta Gut's midsection. He let out a startled grunt and doubled over. Having timed that moment with the opening of the train door, I quickly exited onto the platform and got lost in the crowd of waiting passengers. Revenge was sweet!

This was not my first victory over a pasta-padded pervert. On my first trip to Italy some creep had insinuated his firm package into my backside on a crowded bus, but I wasn't in an amorous mood. It was a transgression that I just couldn't let go unpunished.

The guy stood so close behind me that I was able to grind the heel of my shoe into his foot, which also resulted in a rewarding grunt. I had always been told that things like that happened to single girls on buses in Italy – in other words, it's a custom, just deal with it – but my response was no thanks! A girl traveling on her own had to have some moxie.

Touring Paris by myself was a great adventure, but I couldn't wait to get to Toulouse. On our last night in Paris Gigi hit the town for one last wild ride. I stayed in the room listening to music on Joseph's record player. We had a flight at 1:30 PM the next day, and I wanted to be fresh after nearly a week of nonstop cafés and sightseeing by day and clubbing by night.

I was just drifting off to sleep on the narrow cot when Joseph came back from an outing. By then I was somewhat conversant in basic French. I hoped that he would just sleep on the floor as he had before, but this time, he squeezed himself onto the tiny cot next to me and began touching and kissing me.

"Joseph, I'm sorry, but I don't want to," I ventured in French, fully aware that this six-foot tall, well-muscled man could have just overpowered me right on the spot.

"Non?" he asked, somewhat quizzically. And I said, "Oui – non," in a silly way, but he got the point and thankfully slid onto the floor. I always appreciated that he was a complete gentleman; the guy could have raped me right then and there, but he was respectful. Some things were going well after all.

If Pluto had had any destructive designs on me that way, something more powerful thwarted them. It was a difficult summer, but things never stooped to that level of physical violence, and I was grateful for that.

The next morning's fare was a mix of agitation and anger. We had tickets for a 1:30 PM flight from Orly to Toulouse, but it was already close to noon with no Gigi in sight. As the clock ticked away I became more and more incensed. We still needed to call a taxi, get to the airport, check the luggage, and board the plane. After noontime came and went I totally lost it.

If Pluto was ever going to split the atoms that were whirling around in my brain, it was at that moment. I couldn't contain my jealousy and my frustration with her behavior any longer. In a sudden fury I scooped up all of Gigi's clothing, shoes, and jewelry and unceremoniously flung them into her suitcase.

She finally drifted in around 12:30. The ticking time bombs kept going off.

"Where the hell have you been? We have a 1:30 flight and we still have to find a cab!" She saw her suitcases in disarray on the floor and immediately became incensed.

"What the hell have you done with my stuff?" She jerked open her suitcase and began to rearrange the items that I had angrily flung inside them.

"You threw my jewelry in here like this? It's all tangled together. This is a mess!"

ANYWHERE BUT HERE: CONFESSIONS OF A PISCES MOON

"No, you're a mess. We're going to miss the flight because you couldn't get your lazy ass out of some fool's bed! You knew we had a 1:30 flight!"

Back and forth we went. It was a delicious release of all my pent-up frustrations. We bickered all the way in the cab to Orly, only to learn that we had missed our flight.

"Oh great, Gigi, that's just great!" I complained. She remained aloof and silent. Fortunately we were able to board the next flight and we arrived at her mother's still in good time for dinner.

Gigi was not completely unaware of how her behavior impacted me. At her mother's apartment we had to share a bedroom with two small beds in it. Finally I could be alone with her and hopefully share a few private moments. But then, more combustible designs prevailed.

As scary as it felt, I decided to reveal my feelings. Gigi had questioned me about being gay in the past; she knew that I was gay even before I could fully admit it to myself. But now was the time of bitter reckoning. She was always quick to nip things in the bud, no matter how unpleasant; this time she may as well have removed my heart with a hacksaw.

"Look, you know I care about you, and I know you want to sleep with me, but it's not gonna happen."

Pow. In one single blast, Pluto found its mark like a cruise missile. I was beyond devastated. If a trap door could have sprung open beneath my feet at that moment I'd have gladly plunged to the deepest depths of the earth – anywhere to escape the shattering blow of rejection – anywhere but there.

I had hit rock bottom – I could no longer stand by her side like a wounded puppy who got no love from its master. That was it. Dejected as I felt, I knew I had to get as far away from Gigi and her dangerous liaisons as humanly possible.

This time Fortune heard and answered my prayer – within only days of being in the south of France, Gigi hooked up with a handsome, unassuming French teacher, Jean Pierre, who for a change seemed to have a decent head on his shoulders. And, for a change, he was a responsible, mature Frenchman, a departure from her sleazy norm. I wondered how long that caprice would last.

They quickly fell into the throes of passionate love. The two escaped on a romantic getaway, leaving me behind with Gigi's mother, Marie. It was perfect. My French was improving, which made our visit fun as well as educational. My visit with Marie went a long way toward healing my emotional turmoil.

Marie Bouchard was a portly woman with a dreamy countenance and dishwater-pale complexion whose blue eyes perpetually appeared fixed in the distance, as it there was something else out there far more appealing than anyplace within her immediate reach. She must have been a Pisces.

She was a solitary figure, somewhat eccentric and out of step with everyone around her, but very kind and pleasant nonetheless. We took an instant liking to each other.

In the evenings we sat at her rustic kitchen table and spun stories of our past over decanters of wine fresh from the local vineyards and packs of Gauloise and Marlboro cigarettes. On the table lay a worn French-English dictionary that helped me butcher the French language just enough to make myself understood.

Marie and I talked about everything – my friends, marriage, the Church, social problems - nothing was off limits, and my budding French got a good workout. I spent a full two weeks with her, which passed quickly; I actually began to relax and enjoy myself. My plan was to ride by train all the way down to the Riviera, then east to the northern border of Italy, arriving at Emma's home in Bergamo by way of express train from Milan.

After six weeks of navigating tense sexual liaisons, a harrowing identity crisis, a woeful sense of abandonment, and a demoralizing rejection, I was finally moving on to the land of my ancestors, where all my recent sorrows, like them, could hopefully dissolve into the past.

I had grown quite attached to Marie during my visit, and our goodbye was especially bittersweet. For my departure Marie had kindly booked me a coach on the overnight express train to Milan which departed Toulouse at 11 PM. At 10:30 she packed my suitcase onto her little moped, and with me riding behind her we made our way to the train station. I embraced her and headed slowly up the platform, savoring my last moment in France with mixed emotions.

After boarding the train I turned for a final wave goodbye. Marie stood forlornly and waved farewell. I thought I saw her wipe a stray tear or two from her face, then turn and ride away. She had given me sustenance and shelter from a storm of emotional chaos, and I always remembered her kindness and her companionship. I never saw her again, but I never forgot her. We exchanged letters one Christmas, but sadly I wasn't able to decipher out her scrawled handwriting. A few years ago I heard that she passed away, and fond memories transported me back to her modest kitchen, the two of us laughing over cabernet and cigarettes.

By the time I left Italy the summer was half done and so was I. I had hoped to embark on a thrilling journey of discovery through the villages and vineyards of France with my French companion; instead, I had plunged into an abyss of confusion and despair. It was a journey, all right, more like a rocky whitewater tumble across the River Styx, eyes wide open, than a leisurely paddleboat ride down the River Seine.

I was totally alone, and not just in my thoughts. I was a party of one on a strange continent of millions, no one knew me, and there was no one to talk to. It was expensive to telephone home, and telegrams cost money. And had I called home, what would I have said?

"Mom, guess what, I'm gay."

"Mom, we slept on the floor with strange men in Paris."

"Dad, I punched a guy on the Paris Metro."

"Dad, I'm in love with a nymphomaniac."

Silence was definitely my best option.

There was nothing I could say even if I had someone to talk to. It wasn't a question of talking; it was a question of listening within for the answers. Fortunately, I never minded my own company. Although I felt betrayed and lonely, my solitude provided a welcome retreat from the chaos I had just left behind.

In the midst of crisis I have always been resourceful, probably thanks to my heavily Scorpionic eight-house chart. For the journey I had brought two cameras with me - a little plastic Instamatic and a super-8 movie camera. Disgusted by how matters were going here on earth, I turned my gaze skyward and began to take photographs – of castles on high, of the majestic Alps, of magnificent cathedrals spiraling upward to the heavens, of spectacular sunsets over the rugged Italian landscape.

Photography turned my attention outward, away from my own inner angst. And the spectacular evidence of a gloriously rich civilization still lay at my feet for the taking. Focusing outward became the operative word – pun intended.

CHAPTER SEVEN
ARRIVEDERCI, ITALIA

That midnight train ride through the Riviera opened a whole new window on my summer of discontent, along with a show of spectacular scenery from my window seat. As dawn broke across the horizon the train fast approached the Riviera, where the train tracks ran quite close to the shore, presenting a mesmerizing view of the dazzling buildings along the coast of Monte Carlo, the luscious Mediterranean shimmering in the background. I was spellbound. Finally a chance to reconnect with some semblance of peace.

As we descended the train for the passport check at Ventimiglia I inhaled several refreshing lungfuls of cool Alpine air. With six weeks still to go, I would be free of the curse of Gigi and back in my beloved ancestral land. My long-awaited trip was finally going to materialize exactly the way I had hoped and imagined.

But not for long. On August 2, 1971, Mars entered a retrograde phase in Aquarius – friends were going to be downright tricky, if not hostile – plus, this Mars was attacking my twelfth house of secret enemies.

But the secret enemy was quick to make herself known. I had no sooner settled into a relaxing visit with my pen pal in Bergamo when upsetting word came by way of a telegram.

It was from Gigi. Marie had innocently given her my Bergamo address, and Gigi had written to announce that she was en route to Italy with her latest paramour, Jean-Pierre, who had somehow managed to survive three full weeks in her tumultuous company. I was completely mortified. They were due to arrive the very next day and, to my immense chagrin, intended to take a cab to my friend's house after their arrival by train. This news hit me like a runaway Ferrari on the fast-paced M1, "Highway of the Sun," but more aptly named Highway to Hell.

While in Marie's company I had deliberately skirted any discussion of the trouble I was having with Gigi, unwilling to upset her about her daughter's crazy behavior. But my secrecy had backfired in my face.

Marie did not know that by going to Italy I was deliberately distancing myself from Gigi; she thought nothing of giving my Bergamo address to her daughter. My well-intentioned discretion had led to another debacle of that summer – what could possibly go wrong next?

If ever there was a time that I wished I could have teleported a cell phone back to the past, this was it. Or rather, teleported myself all the way back to the States. I had not invited Gigi to Italy; she had invited herself and Jean-Pierre as well, and was about to again ruin my plans. I could just imagine my Italian friends' reaction upon their uninvited visit. I was certain that her trim, mini-skirted legs and skin tight, low cut dresses would mortify my friends and all their neighbors, who would no doubt take delight in running such a hot item through the local gossip mill – all at my unsuspecting friend's expense.

Italians, or Europeans for that matter, were not yet wearing jeans and t-shirts in the early 1970s; they still dressed somewhat conservatively when going out in public, and women did not wear tight, revealing clothing with plunging necklines and thigh-high dresses. Gigi's dress style then is nothing scandalous now, but in those days it certainly raised a few eyebrows. She was a woman well ahead of her time.

With frustration bordering on insanity I realized that the situation had to change drastically. I would go off with Gigi and Jean-Pierre and leave my friends in peace, free from her disruptive behavior. It hadn't dawned on me to just send the two of them packing as I probably should have done. My hopelessly Piscean desire to try and make something fragrant out of a stinking shit pile took over.

And that Piscean trait could be quite forgiving – in spite of it all I still harbored a soft spot in my heart for Gigi. Insane as it sounds, I still hoped for some fantastical chance of a loving reunion.

Some days later, Mercury, transiting my seventh house in Virgo, would also go retrograde, adding even more pandemonium to an already maddening seventh-house type scenario. That calm, peaceful summer dream reverted to the stuff of cold sweaty nightmares.

Reluctantly but resolutely, I gathered up my belongings, bid my friends a sad and premature addio, and took off for parts unknown and uncharted with the ungainly French lovers in tow. We hitchhiked and bussed our way down to a charming little seaside town near Genoa by the name of Fiascherino, which offered a secluded private beach that we invaded every day.

Happily, Jean-Pierre, perceptive gentleman that he was, intuited my ravaged emotions about Gigi. He, too, had sensed a turbulence about her that troubled him, and in her absence we would talk it over in my halting French. Like Marie before him, he and I became close confidantes during that trip, and we corresponded for quite some time after I returned home. I still have his beautifully written letters in a scrapbook.

Like me, he had been smitten by Gigi's seductiveness and carefree ways and, like me, he too would eventually fall victim under her swift sword stroke of rejection. But, like Marie, I had gained a caring companion and a dear friend. As callous as Gigi was toward me, she often managed to steer me into the company of loving friends who rescued me from the ill effects of spending too much time with her.

The rest of that trip is a blur in my memory, probably because it ran so counter to what I had hoped it would be. At the end of August I reversed course and headed back to Gatwick Airport, the starting point of the whole debacle, and boarded the charter flight back to New York. I don't to this day even remember Gigi being there. I had long ago given in to the utter defeat of the trip being ruined, time and again, by my decision to travel with her.

But who ever suspected that Mr. Jekyll would morph into Mr. Hyde until he had already done so? I had had no warning about Gigi's penchant for promiscuity throughout that entire school year. Had I been aware of astrology then, I would never have traveled with her. Then again, maybe it was in the stars – I came away with an entirely new identity and a deeper understanding and awareness of myself. That precarious leap into adulthood rarely ends in a smooth landing.

All was not lost that torturous summer. I had discovered a new talent that I took great pleasure in – photography. I had no idea where this new pursuit would lead, but when I returned home I had bundles of photos and home movies to share. One frequent visitor to my dorm housing, Ken, a senior journalism major at Rutgers, took a strong interest in my photography.

"These are really, really good pictures. You have something there."

"I just used a little Instamatic camera, nothing special."

"No, but they show that you have a good eye for composition. The camera doesn't matter. Your photographs are well-balanced, thoughtful, and they tell a story." I was impressed.

A teacher at Rutgers also watched my Super 8 movies, most of which featured Gigi, the leading lady, sauntering around in her bikini on a beach in La Spezia. She did a command performance, lithely strolling across the sand, her graceful body backlit by the late afternoon sun. The scene delivered a delicate stroke of sensuality. But I was aghast at the teacher's observation.

"You are in love with this girl." My jaw dropped; I was shocked that my work had given my secret away so easily. But it was there for the seeing. I had captured Gigi in a very sensuous, romantic way, and it came across through my film work.

And it made sense: natal Neptune conjoins my Mercury-Venus-Sun stellium and sextiles midheaven Mars. I can be creatively productive when not feeling totally delusional or confused, which back then was pretty much a fifty-fifty proposition – or maybe, 60-40. Photography was waiting for me in the wings, but first I had to deal with a number of pressing matters, especially, my health, both physical and mental.

The stressful summer had left a mark on my psyche and my physique as well; I had lost weight, I was pale and shaky, and I had taken to chain-smoking cigarettes. But I returned to my final year at Rutgers on a mission. Gigi was scheduled to be my roommate for that senior year, but that had to change.

At the semester registration I switched my room, and chose as my new roommate an Italian girl who proved to be a great friend throughout that crucial last year of college. Gigi was surprised when I told her I wasn't going to be rooming with her. Apparently she didn't get the memo about how badly things had gone for me during the course of that awful summer abroad. It would have to be too bad.

The second order of the day was even more crucial to my wellbeing: I went to the Student Health Center and signed up for a semester of free psychotherapy. The long, unforgiving crush of Pluto across my seventh house Saturn in Virgo demanded that strong measures be taken to shore up my mental health and my emotional boundaries. Transformative change was not negotiable. I had always been too sensitive and fragile in the face of emotional distress, and I needed to develop better coping skills. And to begin to accept myself on my own terms, and not someone else's – a tall order for an accommodating Libran with a Pisces Moon.

Once home again I had many other things on my emotional agenda as well. One was to reveal my true sexuality to my parents. It took quite a while to summon up the courage to do it, but the outcome was memorable. After stumbling through a timid, halting, speech, I outed myself as a gay woman, waiting for the blowback.

Instead, my parents simply smiled and replied, "That's what we thought." It was all okay. And life went on. We were still a family. Best of all, I never lost a job or got kicked out of my home. And no women ever got attacked in dark alleyways, bathrooms, or elevators.

CHAPTER EIGHT
FROM FACTORY TO PHD

The interminable trudge toward graduation day finally ended in May 1972 and, unbelievably, I chose to celebrate it with Gigi, who had stubbornly but tenuously remained on the periphery of my life that senior year. Gigi was sad that I was going on to graduate while she still had two years left of college. I, on the other hand, couldn't be happier to be moving on, to what, I didn't know – as a Piscean Moon escapist, my actions were more often geared toward getting away from old unpleasant things than moving toward new promising ones. It would be a while before I understood this repeating pattern.

After graduation I spent an eye-opening year in the real world of work. The country was in a recession and there were no jobs. My first official job after graduating with my Bachelor of Arts degree was in a record factory where I stacked up piles of 33 RPM vinyl LPs and slit the plastic jackets off them so that they could be repackaged and returned to market. It paid $1.65 an hour. I worked the day shift, from 7:00 AM to 3:30 PM. If I thought the 8:00 AM classes at Rutgers were hard, I was in for a rough reality check.

The factory forewoman, who could have doubled for an escapee from a psychiatric ward, spent the entire shift bullying and harassing us peons. After four days I walked out in disgust, returning only to pick up my measly paycheck of $52.80. Just days into my post-academic life I was already at odds with the working world.

I then graduated to the job of typist in a machine shop. It paid $2 an hour; I was steadily moving up in the wage-earning world. There was nothing for female college graduates to do in those days besides become a secretary, a typist, a teacher, or God forbid, get married, something that never appealed to me.

Or you could pursue an advanced degree, which would only serve to postpone your entry into a world that still offered little reward for all your academic efforts. I chose to pursue a doctoral degree in Italian literature – at least it would keep me busy studying something I loved while postponing the inevitable dilemma of figuring out where I fit into the world.

With nothing else on the horizon, I defaulted back into academia, another whistle stop on my desultory train ride toward a hazy, uncertain future. But the Universe had grand designs.

In the spring of 1973 I applied to the Italian Department of Graduate Studies at Rutgers, which was at the time the most highly regarded graduate department of Italian literature in the country. I had a near-perfect cumulative average in Italian studies and my professors awarded me a fully paid Henry Rutgers Fellowship toward obtaining my doctorate.

I had no idea what I would do with a PhD in Italian literature but it had to beat typing in an office or slitting the plastic jackets off of records. And the ultimate goal of receiving the PhD was far enough in the distant future to allow me the opportunity to put off making any life-altering decisions for a few more years. Decision by default, how Libran and Piscean can one get?

At grad school I made an extremely important acquaintance. J. Lee Lehman, PhD, world-renowned astrologer, lecturer, teacher, and writer, was also at Rutgers graduate school. We were in different departments but we hung out with the same people and became friends. It's funny because neither of us was into astrology at the time. Before astrology Lee was a scientist, getting her PhD in Botany, but

ANYWHERE BUT HERE: CONFESSIONS OF A PISCES MOON

unbeknown to us, our celestial guardians were preparing to set a change in course.

I was resigned to living a life of malaise; I had done well in school but sensed absolutely no direction in life. Teaching Italian, about the only thing I could do with a PhD, did not resonate with me, and I had no qualifications to become a translator. It was the typical catch-22 situation where you needed experience to get a job, but no one would hire you unless you had experience.

My friends in the Italian Department were struggling mightily to get their PhDs, many of them spending at least seven years at it, and some had actually suffered mental breakdowns because of the stress. That was not the way for me to go, so after a year and a half I left academia for a real job and became a paralegal. The steady hours and paycheck were comforting and I did well at my job, but once I mastered the necessary skills my familiar old nemesis, boredom, began to set in.

I had fallen into a mental paralysis about what to do with my life. The things I loved, like astronomy, the paranormal, and the occult, did not offer entry-level positions of employment. When transiting Saturn made a square to itself at the age of 21 (from tenth house Sagittarius to seventh house Virgo) I was in a state of depression and exhaustion, fueled by the bitter romantic disappointment with Gigi, the inability to find meaningful work, and the lack of any sense of direction.

This youthful malaise makes perfect sense to me now - such huge expectations for a 21-year-old! But I never had much use for patience, and that was a recurring problem. Saturn rules time, which young people have no real concept of until they start running out of it – such are life's ironies, also under Saturn's domain.

CHAPTER NINE
NEPTUNE'S LENS

With a Piscean Moon and four planets in Libra the indecisiveness and procrastination came naturally to me. I drifted passively into the next phase of life as a hard-working but uninspired paralegal, where I slogged away for the next four years. But there was that creative outlet that I had discovered while in Europe but not yet explored. It was time.

One of my co-workers, Mary, was an amateur photographer and took an interest in my photographs of Italy. It brought back to mind Ken's praise and the teacher's astute observations about my film of Gigi. Mary encouraged me to pursue my interest further and got me a discount to buy a "real" camera from a local camera shop where her boyfriend worked.

In February 1975 I purchased a 35mm Pentax single lens reflex camera and began shooting black-and-white photographs. After devouring a few photography books I was off and running. No place was off limits in search of good shots – New York City, the Jersey countryside, even the local garbage dump, a great place to find all manner of soft, harsh, and conflicting surface textures and contrasting lighting. I was hooked.

My garden apartment had a large bathroom that comfortably housed a darkroom. I purchased the equipment and, being a purist, I started from scratch, developing my own film and processing my own photos, even matting and framing them myself.

It was the perfect addiction for my Pisces Moon to swim in Neptune's territory. Every weekend I would spend all night in the darkroom, emerging at 4 or 5 AM with several freshly developed 8 x 10 photographs. I loved every minute of it. I lived for the splash and smell of developer, stop bath, and fixer, and began to experiment with lithographs, underexposures, overexposures, sepia toning, and creative lens coverings like Vaseline or panty hose. The most common items can produce amazing soft focus effects!

People began to take note of my work, and I held two photography exhibits at the Unitarian Church in Princeton, where customers actually bought my art and ordered copies of prints. I had taken some nice color shots of sunsets, including a dazzling one over the Arno River in Florence with Ponte Vecchio in the background.

Something inspirational and deeply satisfying was finally born from those miserable months in Europe. During the intense summer of my discontent Neptune had tossed me a lifeline, and Ken's encouragement had set me in the right direction.

It was happy Jupiter, ruler of my Moon and my tenth house, that fueled the creative drive to pursue photography. That February of 1975 Jupiter was transiting my first house Moon while Neptune crossed my tenth house Sagittarius cusp. But a funny thing happened on the way to the proverbial bank.

I tried to turn photography into a business, which was an unfortunate mistake. I didn't want to do weddings, baby pictures, or graduations and that was how most photographers made their living. Just turning my passion into a day-to-day business began to kill off my creative inspiration, and over time the pressure of trying to monetize the hobby drained me of all enthusiasm. The clock was sadly ticking on my budding but aborted career in photography, and I was losing my grasp on the buoyant enthusiasm that had once fueled my inspiration.

I had not yet reached back out to the stars, but an invitation was waiting in the wings. Relief was in sight, and it would come by way of

ANYWHERE BUT HERE: CONFESSIONS OF A PISCES MOON

two psychics. One was already dead, the other one very much alive, but only barely hanging by a thread onto some semblance of sanity.

CHAPTER TEN
PREDICTIVE PARANOIA

My interest shifted from astronomy to astrology in the Seventies when the New Age movement took hold, turning people on to meditation, mantras and manifestation. Astrology was becoming popular, with people turning to their daily horoscopes for quick tips and insights.

Suddenly astrologers and psychics were filling the airwaves with advice, usually about love, money, and predictions for the future; the magnificent art had become relegated to a parlor game. It was crass commercialization at its finest, or worst, depending on your preference, as I would come to realize later.

Astrology was considered a fortune-telling trick for entertainment purposes only, instead of the powerful guide that it can be. The crass mass and marketing media did it a vast disservice, leveling it to the stature of a cheap party trick. Fortunately, many outstanding career astrologers like Lee Lehman counteracted that trend with their work, providing serious astrologers with essential reference works and teachings.

I especially found it irritating when "what's your Zodiac sign" became a mantra of bar-hoppers too lazy to come up with creative pickup lines of their own. I adopted a permanent response, "I'm a STOP sign!" It put a merciful if not blunt damper on those awkward barstool conversations.

I didn't know much about astrology then, but I was attracted to the occult and always eager to learn new subjects. My sister Cheryl had become friends with a gifted psychic astrologer, Linda, whose piercing, penetrating blue eyes could read people at a glance. Her brash, unfiltered persona sheltered a heart of gold. She took an instant liking to me and as soon as we were introduced she whipped out her Tarot cards – a well worn but colorful Rider-Waite deck – and began to read for me.

"You are a natural born astrologer and you have the gift of reading the cards too. You have an innate understanding of the occult arts because you practiced them in a past life. You have done all this before, many times." The reading left me in awe, but I wasn't surprised. My attraction to the occult is apparent in my birth chart, and that didn't just come out of nowhere. Linda now saw me as a kindred spirit and took to mentoring me in the wisdom of the stars and the mysteries of the Tarot.

She lived in a desolate rural expanse of western New Jersey in a rehabilitated farmhouse accessible only by narrow dirt roads. It was an hour drive to visit her, but I looked forward to my visits with anticipation. What I didn't expect, though, was to be shown coming attractions of Linda's psychic collapse and mental disintegration. That led to the scariest and most eerie night of my life.

I knew that Linda drank and did drugs – a dangerous combination for someone already tuned into other dimensions. Cocaine had not yet hit the streets in force but marijuana, LSD, and mescaline were easily acquired. I also came to suspect that Linda was also doing a bit of dabbling in magick and the dark arts. I knew enough to know that if she didn't tread carefully with her practice there could be severe blowback.

It wasn't wise to play in Neptune's nether regions unless one was very well protected and prepared. For that reason, I kept any idea of practicing ritual white magick at bay. As much as I adored Linda, I sensed that her emotional makeup was not balanced or stable enough to be dabbling in psychic adventurism, and it concerned me.

ANYWHERE BUT HERE: CONFESSIONS OF A PISCES MOON

Over time my sister and I noticed that Linda was experiencing episodes of severe paranoia. She had pushed beyond the veil that separated our world from the chaotic realms that lay in wait for those who are mentally or psychically vulnerable. One of Linda's main complaints was that she was being watched by "the man," that men in suits were hanging around her house and following her – a typical paranoid ideation.

It would take a few decades to realize that she was actually on point about many frightening truths. One disturbing revelation was that we were all being spied on and listened to through our electronic devices. As I sat on her couch one evening she pointed to the television set and said, "There! They are listening through the speakers! And some day they will be tracking us all through electronic devices – you'll see!"

We were still years away from 1984, and further still from the era of computers, cyberspace, and cell phones, but the very thought of Linda's pronouncements sent chills of apprehension down my spine. In some ways she was hitting the nail on the head years before most people had any inkling that such covert activities would even be possible. And this was before the coming of AI and all the devices that spy on and track people in their everyday activities.

Things finally came to a terrifying head. I recount this story knowing full well that it may be met with some skepticism, but if you have read this far, there's a strong chance you will believe me. And as bizarre as it sounds, this account is the honest truth.

I visited Linda on one warm spring evening in 1978. We had no sooner sat down to do some readings when she began to regale me with stories of crazy incidents going on in her house. First, she had noticed weird clicking sounds over the phone line, then, lights flashing in her house, and finally, cars driving past her farmhouse slowly and deliberately, as if scoping the place out.

They were not average run-of-the-mill cars but large, black vehicles with blacked-out windows, like the imposing SUVs that the three-letter agency spooks drive around in today. We were always being spied on through her television set or stereo speakers so we had to watch what we said. A weird atmosphere pervaded the home that no burning of candles or incense could alleviate.

That night Linda's paranoid accounts were getting to me. Suddenly we both heard something moving in front of her house. Linda jumped up from her seat and rushed to the window, peering through the drawn blinds.

"There! There they are, there they are watching us!"

To my shock, I looked outside and noticed a long, white limousine parked in front of her house. Once she opened the blinds it slowly pulled away and sped down the dirt road, stirring up clouds of dust. A long, white limousine with tinted windows lurking on a dirt road in the middle of rural New Jersey on a Saturday night?

"That was them!" she cried. "You saw them. That's what I've been telling you about." I couldn't light a cigarette fast enough; my fingers trembled trying to strike the match. Now I was genuinely terrified.

"But what do you do, what can you do if you know they're watching you?" I implored, realizing that maybe these incidents were not just the result of some paranoid delusion.

"You have to send them a thought form that you know what they're up to and you're not afraid."

"Not afraid" was the operative phrase. This was way scarier than any horror story I had ever heard around the proverbial campfire.

ANYWHERE BUT HERE: CONFESSIONS OF A PISCES MOON

It was now after midnight, and I was faced with the daunting task of driving home through the countryside on unlit, remote dirt roads – what had I been thinking staying out there so late? I was too terrified to drive but could not muster the courage to ask Linda if I could crash at her house; I would in any case still have to make that long drive home.

So with trembling hands I bid Linda an uncertain goodnight, and made a fast exit to my car, keys jangling in my shaky fingers. Above me the night sky registered pitch dark, moonless, and foreboding. Distant, unrecognizable animal sounds punctuated the eerie silence.

I cruised gingerly through the dirt roads without incident, but once I reached the main road my worst fears materialized. The road was empty, but only for a moment. Suddenly and seemingly from nowhere a car raced up from behind and began tailgating me, nearly bumper to bumper, with its high beams on. The beams fully illuminated the interior of my car, flashing circles of light off my dashboard. Shit, I am being followed! Linda was right!

This harassment continued for several minutes, with the car behind me driving threateningly close to my rear bumper. I tried at first to shake him off, but when I swerved he swerved with maniacal deliberation. The palms of my hands, now sweaty, began to slip on the steering wheel. All I could think of was what Linda had told me, "Send them a thought form, so that they know you know they are there, and that you're not afraid."

I had played games with mental telepathy before, but this was no game – both cars continued to fly forward, nearly bumper to bumper, at 60 mph with my pursuer showing no signs of letting up. At that moment a weird thought flashed through my mind, and before I even knew it, I was mentally broadcasting the message "I'm going to get my gun."

I don't know where that crazy thought came from. I didn't have a gun. But my pursuer's high beams brightly lit up my dashboard, where any movements I made could easily be seen. Slowly and deliberately I reached over and opened my glove compartment, as if to reach for a gun. At that precise moment the pursuing car suddenly screeched its brakes and swerved crazily out of the lane onto a nearby off ramp, disappearing into the pitch darkness. It was over!

It had worked. Linda's solution, however demented or paranoid, had worked! And I made it safely home in one piece, albeit a bundle of nerves. I had to leave all the lights on throughout that sleepless night, and for days afterward I couldn't get that freaky incident out of my mind.

That was the last time I ever visited Linda. I learned shortly thereafter that she suffered a mental collapse and was spending time in a rehab center. But who were those people in that sleek white limousine, and who had tailgated me so closely for several miles on that deserted highway? It was one time where I preferred to believe in coincidences.

The lesson driven home was, don't play in the chaotic realms. The dark arts are nothing to dabble with, especially if your psychic energy field is already weakened by drinking or drugs. I have never forgotten that lesson, but Linda, who had helped me by example, sadly could not help herself.

By summer of 1978 I was about to embark on a new adventure, one that would move me south to a charming colony of independent thinkers. Neptune would continue her trek across my house of career, but this time, the direction was southward, and much further outward – from garbage dumps and sunsets to the skies and their vast horizons beyond.

CHAPTER ELEVEN
EDGAR AND THE BEACH

That summer of 1978, just months after the bizarre tailgating incident, I did something totally out of character – I made a life-altering decision on the spur of the moment. It was a first in the life of an indecisive multiple Libran with a vacillating Pisces Moon. And it was unforgettable.

My sister Cheryl was moving to Virginia Beach to study the readings of psychic trance medium Edgar Cayce and asked if I wanted to join her. I went all in at once without a moment's thought. The Edgar Cayce Foundation, also called the Association for Research and Enlightenment or ARE, was a well-known institute dedicated to spiritual teachings and development. It was an exceptional opportunity for me to expand my knowledge of metaphysical subjects.

And for once I wasn't alone. The Virginia Beach of the late Seventies was the East Coast's answer to San Francisco - a teeming colony of spiritual seekers, astrologers, psychics, mediums, metaphysical healers, artists, and some hippies left over from the Sixties. At last I was in my element.

Occult-minded and metaphysical people and literature were everywhere, and I inhaled the atmosphere like laughing gas. I put pedal to the metal to finally indulge my fascination with astrology, the occult, the Tarot, and just about anything else within those realms.

Edgar Cayce (1877-1945) was a psychic trance medium who gave tens over 14,000 readings from the early to mid Twentieth Century. He simply lay on a couch, went into deep trance, and answered questions sent in by various clients who sought advice pertaining to problems of health, finances, business, family issues, social conditions, and the like.

His accuracy in diagnosing medical ailments was uncanny, given that he lacked a formal education, and his recommendations for treatment helped tens of thousands of people. His medical and metaphysical readings are the most widely researched and published psychic documentation of the Twentieth Century.

Gladys Davis Turner was his secretary, and I had the great pleasure of meeting her. For many years she sat by his side and dutifully transcribed the contents of all of the sessions, which she then typed and entered into huge notebooks.

Although the readings leaned heavily toward physical and emotional disorders, there was no subject that Cayce did not speak on. The Cayce readings dealt with topics ranging from health to ancient history to the future; he discussed World War II, aliens, earth changes, the stock market, business, and the Bible. Nicknamed "the Sleeping Prophet," scholars and seekers continue to research and write about the Cayce readings today.

Cayce also spoke a great deal on astrology. There was my invitation! I was surrounded by new knowledge, and I couldn't get enough – astrology, psychic healing, spiritual disorders, bodily energies, mental attitudes. Cayce always said, "Mind is the Builder" – a maxim that I would learn, forget, and then re-learn time and again. Hadn't I already noticed such advice on that London double-decker bus?

I'm a Libran with four planets in Libra, all in trine aspect to Jupiter rising in Aquarius, so I know all about excessive mental activity. My mind has no "off" switch – it's a busy builder for good and sometimes, not so good. In Virginia Beach the Universe was continuing to reinforce its message that it had dropped on me in the entrance to that

ANYWHERE BUT HERE: CONFESSIONS OF A PISCES MOON

double-decker bus in London – "Mind Your Head." It's the reminder of what should become a life-long discipline, one that requires constant repetition and practice.

The Cayce readings inspired me to embark on a course of total self-improvement by following a healthy regimen of diet, daily exercise, prayer, meditation, massage, chiropractic, and hydrotherapy. The most demanding discipline of all was always to mind my mental builder.

Dreams were important too, as they contained messages from the divine. Following Cayce's recommendation I also kept close track of my dreams in a journal. In October 1978, after only one month at the Beach, I had the mother of all haunting dreams, in vivid Technicolor, no less.

I was in a hot, steamy climate, surrounded by jungle foliage. Crowds of scantily dressed people were standing around in an open field, and they were raising white Styrofoam cups to their lips and then passing out and falling to the ground. There was poison in the cups and the people were all falling down dying or dead – men, women, and children. I awoke in a very disturbed state, and immediately recorded the dream in my journal.

About a month later, the Reverend Jim Jones and some 900 followers from his People's Church enacted the very visions I had seen in this dream in the jungle nation of Guyana. When news of the mass suicide/murder reached me I was beyond shocked. Nebulous Neptune, who had been sailing through my career house for already some time, was making an announcement: I had strongly positive psychic abilities that could, if so desired, be developed into sustainable work.

But I was too timid to fully embrace my psychic side, afraid to lose some semblance of mental control over things (which was just an illusion), afraid of what other shadows it might expose me to. Wired by six placements in air signs, at the end of the day I was still dancing to the incessant beat of my left brain's ceaseless logic-based chatter. For the time being Neptune's message, and gift, would remain adrift at to sea, with the promise of more premonitive dreams sinking slowly beneath the depths.

I have only recently learned through the work of some gifted researchers that the Guyana victims were not all poisoned; many were also shot. It's interesting that the dream paralleled the news and not the full reality of what actually took place, but this does not negate the dream, which was simply telling me something I was about to hear via the news media.

That October dream was timely in view of the fact that Neptune and Mars were swimming through my Sagittarian tenth house all that winter of 1978, and transformer Pluto was passing over my natal Neptune in Libra. It was the winter of Neptune for sure – I lived across the street from the ocean, I studied all kinds of ethereal subjects, I kept a dream journal, I practiced music on my guitar, and I began to visualize a future filled with bright possibilities.

The Cayce library was a magical wonderland for the bibliophile like myself, replete with all manner of literature on spiritualism, the occult, healing, the paranormal, astrology, reincarnation, and all those ethereal things that appealed to me. My sister Cheryl and I lived just a brief walk from the ARE, which the locals fondly referred to as "the R."

We were blessed to be able to rent a small bungalow across the street from the ocean, an expense that would be astronomical now, but affordable back in the late Seventies when "the Beach" was still relatively unknown except for those seeking Enlightenment at the Association.

ANYWHERE BUT HERE: CONFESSIONS OF A PISCES MOON

My sister and I took to studying astrology seriously, and we were in the exact right place for it. Astrologers in town gave lectures and classes and we quickly grew a small clientele of friends. We took our lessons mainly from local astrologers and from a wonderful little book on astrology by Isabel Hickey, *Astrology, A Cosmic Science*.

Soon enough, we jumped right into giving readings for friends, billing ourselves as "the Salerno Sisters." It worked well – when I didn't know something, my sister would, and as fellow Librans, we counter-balanced each other nicely.

Our readings with clients gave me an idea of how a professional astrologer would work. As much fun as the readings were, behind the levity I felt the need to provide support and guidance. This drove home the sheer weight of responsibility that the work entailed; you had to be friend, confidant, confessor, and professor all at once, and you had better know what you were talking about.

Astrology was serious business in more ways than one. In order to erect a chart we had to do all our own calculations by hand, which required three thick books filled with sidereal times, longitudes, and latitudes, and lists of all the time zones in all the cities and countries. Forget about computers; we couldn't even get hold of pocket calculators, which were quite expensive when they first came out.

You couldn't cast a chart without knowing whether the birth took place in a time zone that required adjustment of the exact time of birth. It was a complex operation. This meticulous math surely eliminated many aspiring astrologers as potential practitioners until computerized charts came along sometime in the early Eighties. Even then, those were not completely satisfactory – imagine asking a pressing horary question and having to wait two weeks for the computerized chart bearing the answer to arrive by snail mail! Many times the question would resolve itself before the mail even arrived.

Laboring over those calculations, pencil in hand, was much like what my father endured while cooped up in the tail of his B29 bomber, scanning the night sky over the South Pacific Ocean, sweating over the coordinates, mapping them, correcting the flight course, trying to get it all right. For me at least it wasn't a question of surviving a war! The tradition of astrology surely had been embedded somewhere in our family DNA. In the not too distant future I would come to marvel at the extensive knowledge passed down to us from the ancient astrologers who labored without benefit of all the so-called user friendly materials we now have access to.

Nice things were happening to me in Virginia Beach. Uranus, transiting my eighth house, laid before me as much astrology information as I could hope for. Neptune, with its slow turn through my Sagittarian tenth, ushered in a much more spiritual outlook on life, and I discovered a new type of music based on healing frequencies. Just a month or two into my Virginia Beach experience another blessing came my way, and it afforded me an opportunity to learn the Cayce readings very well.

The small three-bedroom bungalow shared by Cheryl and me was a gift, costing only $225 a month – cheap even by late Seventies standards. I was collecting unemployment checks that the State of New Jersey kindly mailed me every two weeks, and we made some extra cash giving astrology readings. But money was still tight.

We managed to scrape by until a fantastic opportunity came my way. Tom Johnson, who managed the iconic Heritage Health Food Store, was writing an encyclopedia of Edgar Cayce readings for mass-market publication and Tom, who had quickly become a friend of ours, knew I was looking for work.

Tom graciously hired me as a part-time research assistant for the book. I was responsible for researching some three hundred Cayce health

ANYWHERE BUT HERE: CONFESSIONS OF A PISCES MOON

readings and writing synopses of them. I was thrilled – I would be paid for something I was doing anyway, and I got to learn an enormous amount about the workings of holistic and spiritual healing. It paid $3 an hour under the table, and I could do as many or as few hours a week as I wanted until the three hundred readings were finished. It was a perfect arrangement.

The final manuscript was entitled *The Edgar Cayce Encyclopedia* and it went to publication in 1984. It's out of print now, but the book bears my name on the Acknowledgments page. It was an honor to have participated in that huge effort.

Little did I know then that someday I would once again venture into the world of publishing to promote an arcane art whose early lessons I received courtesy of Edgar Cayce and my astrology teachers at the Beach.

As much as I resonated with Virginia Beach, the research project ended after ten months, as did my unemployment, and our cottage was going on the market as a summer rental, well above our affordable monthly payment. Unless I wanted to be a waitress or a hotel maid there were no suitable jobs. I was nowhere near ready to try a career in astrology, so with a heavy heart I returned home to New Jersey.

My sister Cheryl did land a job, and remained at the Beach for many years afterward. She was hired as an editor for the Association for Research and Enlightenment Press, and had the unique opportunity to work with many renowned Cayce researchers and authors. She also got to edit many dozens, if not hundreds, of manuscripts, and gained a profound knowledge of the Cayce material and many other metaphysical practices.

In fact, we went on to follow similar paths as a result of our exposure to the Cayce work. Cheryl also became a massage therapist, later studied

Quantum Touch and other holistic modalities, and now works with anti-aging technology, remote healing, and biofield restoration. It works – I should know – we share a home now and I am one of her best clients!

CHAPTER TWELVE
NEW YORK MINUTES

Readjusting to life in New Jersey was a shock to the system. I went from the leisurely days of strolling the beach and perusing the Cayce library to a fast-paced paralegal job for an intellectual property law firm in midtown Manhattan, an hour's commute by train from my apartment. The energetic change in my environment shot from zero to a hundred in a New York minute.

But I loved working in the City and thrived on the buzz of energy it had to offer. There were occult bookstores and unique metaphysical shops that offered astrology classes there too, so I did not skip a beat in my educational pursuits.

Someone else also landed in the City – my old Rutgers pal, Lee Lehman, who was then working as a scientist at a laboratory on the East Side. We quickly reconnected. As fate would have it we were both studying astrology by then too.

After work I would often stroll down to her East Side apartment for dinner or a drink. We would sit on pillows on the floor of her living room and talk astrology and occult subjects late into the wee hours. Blessed with a genius I.Q. Lee has an amazing mind and seemingly endless capacity for knowledge. We were of like mind on many subjects, but my lazy, namby-pamby Libra/Pisces was no match for her enterprising triple Virgo energies; her work ethic far outpaced mine when it came to serious study and application. It was never any wonder to me that she rose to the top of the astrology profession as she did, and deservedly so.

Lee cultivated a habit that I wish I had also done back then, one that I encourage all students of astrology to do now. She diligently collected the birth data of everyone she knew, from bosses to co-workers to friends and relatives, carefully observing and noting their behavior.

This was an excellent learning tool, with observation being the operative word. I, on the other hand, wiled away much of my silly Libran energy trying to find out if a prospective paramour had Mars-Venus signs compatible to mine. What can I say – it was the Seventies!

With several planets in Leo, Lee proved to be a loyal friend, always there at the right time. On one especially dim-witted evening I went out clubbing in Greenwich Village - always in search of that elusive Mars-Venus connection - and met up with a very interesting young woman – or so I thought.

We got cozy in the bar and decided to take a cab together to her place uptown. Once inside the cab, though, my new friend, who had made a suspicious stop in the bathroom before we left the bar, suddenly decided to release her inner psycho by turning belligerent and hostile. Sensing the influence of drugs, I didn't dare travel another mile with her.

By the grace of God, the cab at that moment just happened to be passing within a few blocks of Lee's apartment. The driver knew something weird was going on and screeched to a quick stop when I asked him. I flung myself out of that cab and ran like a crazy person to the nearest pay phone. It was nearly 2 AM but luckily Lee answered the phone and invited me to crash at her place – psycho disaster averted, thanks to a good friend and some divine timing.

Strange things can, and did, happen when you hang out in bars like I did back in those days. Gay bars were plentiful in New York City, and I

ANYWHERE BUT HERE: CONFESSIONS OF A PISCES MOON

had my fill of crazy escapades similar to this one but not as threatening. I credit my lucky Jupiter rising with the blessing of protection I've always seemed to have. That, of course, did not enhance my decision-making, which was astronomically poor at times. It just took the edge off the consequences of going with the wrong people, like the time I experimented with "boilermakers" – chasing shots of whiskey down with beer after beer, and ending up comatose in a West Village flophouse.

Lee eventually left science to pursue a full-time career in astrology and moved west to San Francisco. I missed having an astrology buddy around and drifted away from my studies. Astrology's light had begun to dim, but as divine timing had it, Lee would resurface some years later, and toss me a much-needed lifeline back into the world of the stars.

The predictable had happened once again. Boredom had begun to set in after only a couple of years in New York. I was looking for my Piscean escape hatch, open to anything that would take me far away from the corporate rat race.

Fitness and exercise clubs had become all the rage, and many of them employed massage therapists. The Cayce readings emphasized the importance of massage therapy, and I enjoyed working with my hands. One day my sister Cheryl called and got an earful of my complaints about how unfulfilling my corporate work was. Like her offer to go to Virginia Beach, she again presented me with an option that I couldn't refuse.

"You could have your own business doing massage therapy. Why don't you go to massage school?" I jumped at the idea. The Swedish Institute of Massage was on W. 28th Street, not far from my office job in Times Square. I asked my boss to allow me to work flex hours to accommodate the massage class schedule and he agreed.

In the fall of 1982 I enrolled in an intensive ten-month training course at the Swedish Institute of Massage in New York City. Swedish massage was considered a serious therapeutic modality and the course was rigorous, requiring studies in anatomy, physiology, and human pathology. The training would provide me with the skills to perform therapeutic and medical massage, thus offering me a ticket out of dry corporate legal work into the thriving field of holistic healing.

It would also allow me the opportunity to create my own business. Even now the therapeutic benefits of massage are greatly underrated and unfortunately, it still carries with it the stigma of "massage parlor" sleaze, as I unfortunately would soon find out.

The stars were aligned with my decision: When I applied to the school Venus, my ruling planet, was transiting Cancer in my sixth house of health; Mars was passing through Scorpio in my eighth, as was nearby Jupiter, and Saturn was about to make a fateful passage across my eighth house Libra stellium – the heavens were setting the stage for new experiences in the field of healing and personal transformation.

Heavyweight Pluto was also having a say in the matter. On the heels of Saturn mowing down my Libra stellium of Neptune-Mercury-Venus like a thicket of weeds, Pluto had rumbled its way across those same planets. The two behemoths were fixing for a showdown, and it was aimed directly at my Libran Sun.

Just two months after the start of massage school, my Libran Sun would meet a heavy Saturn-Pluto conjunction head-on. It had nothing to do with massage school but everything to do with a life-altering accident, one that would strangely end up providing more help than harm.

CHAPTER THIRTEEN
COLLISION COURSE

Astrology studies had drifted into the background, but I still kept abreast of planetary activities. I knew that my life was headed for some very deep-seated and inalterable changes. But this wasn't a Mars transit where you just don't leave the house for a day or two. This was a slow dance between two heavies and I couldn't remain housebound for weeks.

This Saturn-Pluto dance was in an air sign, and I hoped it might have more to do with reshaping my mental structure than my physical one. I was half right. My attitude changed, but as the result of the most horrifying accident of my life.

Day Zero of the Saturn-Pluto collision with my Sun occurred on Saturn's day, of course! I spent the day with a friend who had just gotten cable TV installed, and back in 1983 that was the next big thing.

We binge watched MTV music videos all evening until I realized that I had an anatomy quiz the following Monday morning and needed to go over my notes on Sunday. So I declined my friend's offer to sleep over and, at 1:30 AM I hopped into my little Dodge Colt and began the hour-long drive home.

I was heading north on New Jersey's busy Route 1 corridor in the fast lane. Suddenly I had to hit the brakes - an accident up ahead had backed up traffic for several hundred yards. I felt like a sitting duck stopped in the left lane of a busy thoroughfare, and anxiously began to glance in my rear view mirror for oncoming traffic.

Bright white headlights suddenly flashed in my rear-view mirror. Then came the crunching impact of a forceful rear-end collision. The entire scene played out in slow motion, as accidents strangely tend to do.

I went airborne in my seat, striking my head on the ceiling of the car and jamming my knees into the dashboard. The force of the impact sent my eyeglasses flying up and over my head, landing in the rear of the hatchback. The car behind me was hit by the car behind him, and the impact of both cars caused a massive chain collision.

I was shaken, but not injured. When I climbed out of the car what awaited me was right out of a bad horror movie. The driver behind me emerged from the wreckage with his arms and his hair on fire; flames were shooting out from his jacket sleeves and his collar. A small fire had erupted inside his car and quickly spread, spewing flames from the interior.

In my mind's eye I saw an explosion about to occur. I raced toward the drivers ahead of me shouting, "Move your cars, we're going to blow up!"

We had no sooner driven our smashed-up cars onto the shoulder of the highway when the two cars that had struck me erupted into a massive explosion, sending a fireball skyward high above the power lines. One girl was trapped in her car while the others, clothing alight in flames, ran wildly around, waving their arms in pain and panic. It was beyond gut-wrenching. All I could do was stand there helplessly and await the arrival of the police and rescue teams.

The effect of Saturn-Pluto in Libra made its immediate impact. Once queasy and squeamish at the sight of all things flesh-and-blood related, I strangely stood there in a state of detached calm, as if watching a silent movie frame-by-frame. In my recollection there was complete and total silence. I didn't recall any sounds, only the bizarre montage of

ANYWHERE BUT HERE: CONFESSIONS OF A PISCES MOON

frame-by-frame sequences of the fireball and the unfortunate burning victims.

The girl who was trapped in the car could not escape, and died on the scene in front of us. She was only eighteen years old. The carful of teenagers had just left a nightclub, and their carefree night of partying had within seconds come to an agonizing end. I was lucky to have emerged physically safe and sound.

The Saturn-Pluto conjunction in the air sign Libra made profound changes to my perception of suffering. As upsetting as the scene of carnage was, I could bear witness to misery and suffering and not be devastated by it, while still feeling compassion and sorrow for those less fortunate.

This was something entirely new to me. It became critical to me later on when I worked with seriously ill people – traffic accident victims, people with broken bones, missing limbs, cancerous lesions, you name it.

Saturn had restructured my mental approach to devastating events, and Pluto had presented the opportunity. This has come in handy so many times since. It serves me well even now, in my true crime research, when the disgraceful misdeeds that humans inflict upon each other disturb me but don't demoralize me.

I returned to massage classes right after the accident, not feeling the need for time off. Something inside me was different. My studies in anatomy and physiology were no longer making me queasy.

During our anatomy training we routinely had to view photographs of cadavers with parts of their bodies dissected. I could look at a cross-section of a human heart, layers of thigh muscle, or views of a sectioned eyeball and not feel the rising choke of bile in my throat. Saturn-Pluto had put me through a horrible experience, but gave me a stronger perspective through which to process chaotic and upsetting situations.

Massage school was the springboard to learning other healing modalities. After completion of the ten-month course I went on to take certification courses in sports massage, foot reflexology and Shiatsu. I wanted to understand more about the subtle interplay of mind, body, and spirit. My thoughts never strayed far from the Edgar Cayce readings, and I was curious to explore more of the workings of energy within the human body.

I enjoyed working as a massage therapist; I just had trouble finding enough paying regular clients to make a living. Until I could, I moonlighted as a masseuse while continuing my paralegal day job. It was hard to find regular paying clients, so to promote my business I relied on newspaper advertising.

This was not helpful; it mostly attracted breathers and perverts hoping for a more carnal experience than what I intended to provide. Crank calls in response to my ads persisted until I developed the habit of ratcheting up an ear-splitting volume on my radio while placing the phone against the speaker. That pretty much took care of the repeat offenders.

Once again, reality came calling: Few were in the market for either a full-time astrologer or a medical masseuse, at least not enough people to provide the comfortable living that I was seeking. Massage therapy was not a well-known or highly regarded health practice.

I did cultivate a nice side clientele that enabled me to save enough money to buy my first house, but it was a hustle to work two distinctly demanding joba. Little did I know that severe burnout would overtake me in the not-too-distant future, when Saturn would pay me another sobering visit.

CHAPTER FOURTEEN
THE HOUSE OF SICKNESS

After I received my massage license in 1983 the Eighties seemed to whiz by in all their materialistic glory. It took a very long time to build a regular massage clientele and the income was unpredictable, so I reluctantly stayed at my paralegal job. Moonlighting as a massage therapist was physically demanding, and my paralegal job was mentally stressful. I was burning my candle at both ends, cooking up a recipe for a health crisis.

And my priorities had changed. I was a new relationship and with that came a strong desire to buy my first house. So I worked in New York during the day, saw massage clients on nights and weekends, and set aside money for a down payment. Time off was a precious commodity, but life was looking up - until I awoke one morning in the summer of 1987 with a high fever, penetrating chills, and a burning sensation in my throat. It was a struggle to just get out of bed. It must have been a nasty bout of the flu, I thought, a weird thing to catch in the summertime.

It was weird – and it didn't go away. Strange symptom after strange symptom began to manifest all over my body. Red itchy hives the size of kidney beans would mysteriously burst across my chest and stomach after eating seemingly harmless foods. Deep black craters sank underneath my eyes, more like huge sets of luggage than bags. Puffy pouches of edema circled those dark baggy eyes, giving me a ghoulish appearance.

I was too tired to get out of bed but could not fall asleep at night. As exhausted as I was I rarely slept. Painful intestinal distress was a frequent occurrence, as well as all manner of weird body aches and pains.

My spleen was enlarged and extremely tender to the touch. Frequent fevers reached between 100 and 102. I had entered the House of Sickness.

The angry planet Mars was transiting my sixth house of sickness for two months that summer, while Jupiter opposed my Libran planets. Saturn was crossing my tenth house of career, causing delays in my career as I had zero energy for work.

From day to day I could not drag myself out of bed, get dressed, and walk down to the train station for my daily commute. It had become embarrassing to keep calling in sick; I carried a very heavy workload for the law firm and absences were frowned upon.

Finally one day I called my boss and told her that I was sick, I had no idea when I would be well again, and I would need to file for disability. This news was met with tense disapproval by my superiors and it added more emotional stress to an already difficult situation.

The first doctor shrugged his shoulders and called it the flu, the next one said I just needed rest, and my chiropractor was completely baffled. I underwent a lengthy battery of tests, from HIV to Lyme disease to Epstein-Barr virus. Finally, my blood showed an overwhelming amount of titers that confirmed the presence of the Epstein-Barr virus, a nasty debilitating syndrome that some media fool had thoughtlessly termed "the yuppie flu."

The illness showed no signs of letting up for months. I had turned to doctors mainly to provide documentation for my disability claim, but my real faith lay in holistic medicine. I found the perfect doctor, a kindly woman who was familiar with the Edgar Cayce health readings. The landscape was beginning to brighten.

ANYWHERE BUT HERE: CONFESSIONS OF A PISCES MOON

The doctor was a qualified MD with a specialty in nutrition and holistic medicine, and she believed I suffered from much more than Epstein-Barr. She mentioned something like "cytomegalovirus," a scary sounding name that fit a scary pattern of symptoms.

Whatever it was, she told me point blank that I was suffering from a serious auto-immune disease. My system was beyond exhausted, I had no adrenal function, my liver was in toxic overload, my spleen was extremely enlarged, and I had better start implementing some immediate changes to my lifestyle. In other words, strip everything down and change it.

She was right. I had labored for too long at an unfulfilling job that placed constant demands on my mental and emotional energy. The fast-paced New York pressure was losing its excitement. I was gone 12 hours a day yet still moonlighting as a massage therapist nights and weekends, which was physically demanding as well.

I wasn't fulfilled, but had kept grinding away, putting one foot in front of the other, paying the bills, waiting for paychecks, waiting for the weekends and then, waiting for vacations. It was no way to live. The doctor was right. It wasn't time to flip the script – it was time to burn it.

The burnout had begun to manifest when benevolent Jupiter in Aries opposed all my Libran planets over a period of several months earlier that year – I was overdoing it, running on empty and neglectful of keeping the gas tank full. My friend Saturn had now reached my Midheaven, making me focus on just what was missing in my career and my place in the world – which was practically everything of any real value to me. It was the Saturn seven-year itch - making its first square aspect to itself following its return to its natal position.

Saturn's connection to Mars made sure to drained my Mars energy dry that October, and that was when the proverbial rubber met the road. The doctor gave me a stringent regimen, complete with meditation exercises. I embarked on a strict dietary program, including herbs, minerals, juices, raw greens, and vitamin supplements.

I also avoided stress - which meant avoiding work altogether - and stayed home. I spent most days in bed all day while my partner was away at work, and was blessed to have the companionship of our two beautiful Burmese cats and our perky Pomeranian dog. I watched a lot of television with little energy for anything else. There were days when just pushing the channel changer on the remote control felt exhausting, but it was all I could do to lie in bed and watch one television program after the next.

It was a humbling experience, one that leveled me emotionally as well as physically. I didn't know if I would be able work again; I had researched Epstein-Barr and noted that some sufferers ended up in wheelchairs. My previous frivolous crisis of having no life direction paled in comparison to that realization.

To add to Saturn's merciless grind, Uranus was pummeling my Ceres asteroid in the tenth house. I never looked much at asteroids then, but in retrospect that was an extremely significant aspect. Ceres, the caretaker and nurturer, was telling me that I'd better get to healing and nurturing myself. Uranus the rebel was revolutionizing my approach to self-care. I had left the soothing, healing energy of Virginia Beach and adopted the hectic New York lifestyle, and it had burnt my nerve endings to a crisp. I neglected to mind both mind and body, and throw in spirit for good measure.

Fortunately none of my toxicity issues were due to drinking or drugs. I drank only socially, and drugs were never on the menu. Since childhood I had experienced severe reactions to all manner of drugs, and that included a freaky episode of pot-smoking in college that rendered me so totally paranoid that I would not touch the stuff after that.

Cocaine and speed, common party drugs of the day, were naturally out of the question. Still, my liver showed signs of toxicity. Just goes to show you how much the wrong diet, lifestyle, and attitude can fry the liver as much as the usual chemical suspects.

The biggest moment for me was not in the physical discipline of healing, but the mental. My old mentor Edgar Cayce had reminded me so many times in the past, "Mind is the Builder," but I had conveniently neglected it. I really should have snatched that sign "Mind Your Head" from that London double-decker bus.

I was in desperate need of something to pull myself out of the despair of debilitating illness. I was only 37 years old but looked like 57 and felt like 87. My dark wavy hair was greying practically overnight, and the shiny black luggage under my eyes showed no signs of being unpacked. Something had to give.

One day I was lying in bed wondering how the hell I ever ended up in such a sorry state when it dawned on me to recall other times when I was ill. There was the usual run of childhood illnesses, flus, mumps, chicken pox, headaches, infections, and all of them were connected: In the past I had always healed quickly after getting injured or sick. And in spite of my dilemma I did not believe in my heart that I was a sickly person.

That realization was the turning point. I was not sick – I was a healthy person whose body was simply screaming out for change and overhaul, and it had been doing that for some time before I paid any mind to those screams.

I began to visualize myself healthy, having fun doing the things I always loved to do like music, writing, and astrology. My Neptune/Mercury/Venus stellium sextile Mars gave me the ability to visualize, which I put to good use. I imagined myself in a state of health, up and about and as energetic as I used to be. It became a daily ritual, and in time it reaped rewards.

I returned to work a few months later, but I hadn't yet responded to the ultimate ultimatum: More change was needed. This time the message was driven home by a sneaky Neptune who came bearing a slinky garrotte. I wasn't quite out of the woods yet.

All seemed to go well in my new healed state, until it didn't. My natal Jupiter aspecting my Sun likes to give me outbursts of overconfidence and nonchalance in the face of warning. Jupiter is not always an automatic blessing of divine Providence; the jovial giant can wreak havoc in many ways if we are not mindful to pace ourselves. I've always had the foolish notion that once a problem was resolved it would never rear its head again. This blind spot proved dangerous.

The real estate market was booming in the late Eighties, prices were going up, and I began pressuring myself to buy my own home. It became an obsession that overrode all caution regarding my recent bout with poor health, and I launched myself toward this new goal with a head of steam.

The need for my own space had been festering since childhood. I grew up in a small two-bedroom duplex house – that's half a house, to be precise - with only 850 square feet to share between my sister and my parents, whose relations were often tense and strained. I did my Piscean disappearing act many times within those walls, but it was never enough. Apartments would no longer do. I absolutely had to have space, my own special place to call home.

ANYWHERE BUT HERE: CONFESSIONS OF A PISCES MOON

Soon I found a cozy little house built in 1908, a charming Edwardian colonial with natural pine wood floors, original glass windows and woodwork, archways between the rooms, wainscoting, and beautiful scrollwork. It was everything I loved and wanted in an older home. And it was for sale for an attractive price, as it needed some cosmetic touches.

I fell in love with the house and had to have it. It was just a quick walk down the street from our apartment too, a very easy move. I would need only to change the house number in my address. Having healed from my health crisis – or so I thought – I pressed forward to buy this house for myself, my partner Jane, and our pets.

It was important enough that I got a reading from my astrologer, as things were in the midst of upheaval. We discussed my housing obsession, which she explained as the result of my Uranus opposition – natal Uranus was in Cancer and would soon be opposed by transiting Uranus in Capricorn.

My astrologer felt that the urgency of this Uranus opposition was pushing me toward acquiring my very first home. It was also the time when the so-called "mid-life crisis" would come calling. Well, Uranus must have had other excitement in mind, because it so happened that I not only bought a house, I also finally left my job in New York for a job in New Jersey, much closer to home. These life-altering changes occurred at the exact same time, including moving house. It all proved much more taxing on my newly healed body than I had expected.

Change for change's sake is not always the best idea. Once again, I was pushing myself too hard, and the home purchase, job change and house move became costly in more ways than one.

To add insult to injury I was revisited by a frightening early illness: asthma. During the months preceding the house purchase I suffered a very intense attack of asthma, which seemingly came out of nowhere. Transiting Mars was opposing my Libra stellium, at the same time squared by transiting Saturn in Capricorn. I felt the breath being sucked out of me. From that point on I began suffering asthma attacks with increasing frequency.

Later that month Jupiter jumped into the fray, forming a Grand Cross between my Libra stellium, Mars, and Saturn. The asthma attack was a warning that I was not out of the woods yet with the health problems that had put me on disability just a couple of years before. In my mind, the whole viral episode was already well in the past, but the disciplines I had worked so hard at practicing had fallen by the wayside. I hadn't been minding my head or my body, and throw in spirit for good measure.

Asthma was no stranger to me and its return was most unwelcome. I suffered from asthma in early childhood and remembered the toll it took on myself and my family. Early Fifties medicine had little to offer an asthmatic child other than emergency trips to the doctor's office for painful hypodermic injections of adrenalin.

The doctor told my parents that I suffered from EIA: Exercise Induced Asthma. He gave my parents strict instructions that I could not run or play strenuously; I was not allowed to run or ride my bicycle, which was bad news for a restless tomboy like myself.

Naturally I defied these instructions many times, only to be found slumped over the handlebars of my bike, wheezing and gasping for breath, in need of an emergency shot of adrenalin. Fortunately I outgrew the asthma, but it would revisit me with a vengeance many years later, leaving no margin for error.

This time the asthma was different. Severe attacks would often occur in the middle of the night, always around 4 AM, when I would awaken

ANYWHERE BUT HERE: CONFESSIONS OF A PISCES MOON

from sleep gasping for breath. Sometimes I couldn't breathe after eating certain foods. Sometimes just an innocent cough or sneeze would stir an attack of wheezing. I never knew what would incite the next attack.

My general practitioner set me up with inhalers and tablets of theophylline to keep my airway open. I was also placed on steroids. Both drugs had miserable side effects: the theophylline made me nervous and skittish, the steroids made me hungry and hyper. My body became bloated, I gained weight, and my face puffed out in chipmunk style.

All the drugs were necessary, yet I still had problems breathing. Trips to the emergency room became a little too frequent for comfort. My doctor did all he could drug-wise, but the asthma was becoming more and more threatening and the drugs were not keeping it at bay.

It was fortunate that I lived only two blocks from St. Peter's Hospital in New Brunswick, where I quickly became a "frequent flyer" in the local emergency room, often by ambulance in the middle of the night. The asthmatic condition was taking a toll on my family, who dreaded seeing me endure another health crisis.

One uncomfortable aspect of having chronic asthma was the need for frequent injections, IVs, and blood draws. Since childhood I had harbored an extreme fear of injections – back in the Fifties most needles were of the hollow hypodermic variety, nothing like the small "pinch" needles of today. Hypodermics always hurt, and I developed a phobia about them – phobias being nothing new to Piscean individuals.

I could not receive an injection or give blood without passing out right on the floor of the doctor's office. It became a huge problem for me but there was no other way to gauge the efficacy of my asthma medications.

As the asthma became progressively worse, I was subjected to a more painful experience - arterial blood draws.

Arteries run much deeper under the skin than veins, but in order to properly gauge the amount of medication in my blood stream the blood had to be drawn directly from an artery. For this procedure my arm had to be stabilized in order to allow a hollow needle to be driven in deeply enough to pierce the artery wall. This was a painful, but necessary, procedure, and my dread of needles was putting me over the edge. Something had to give. Mind needed to build a way out of this debilitating phobia. I began to visualize receiving injections with ease.

It took time, but gradually I steeled myself to the point where I could actually relax during the blood draws and injections. I stopped passing out and became much calmer. After a while I could handle an injection without having to lie down, having "built" the scenario many times over in my mind.

This ability to overcome trauma was surely the carryover from the tough Saturn-Pluto transit across my Sun years previously. Little did I know what career change lay in the near future, and it would have everything to do with needles. In the years to follow I received professional training in Manhattan and became a licensed acupuncturist! No one has ever been more amazed by that than me.

I wasn't alone with my health issues. Asthma was growing in epidemic proportions in the Nineties, especially among children, who were often seen puffing on their inhalers in public. The big drug companies produced with more and more drugs to combat the problem, but those drugs carried severe provisos if used too frequently. One such drug, albuterol, would nearly become my undoing.

It was April 12, 1992. The giants of the sky were assaulting me from all sides: Mars in early Pisces had just rolled over my Aquarius Ascendant and entered my first house. Mars has always brought me irritations in that position: burns, injuries, minor accidents and scrapes. In Pisces it was about to set a dangerous course regarding overuse of drugs.

Mars was also on its way to crossing my Moon some days later, but other planets had quicker designs. Saturn in Aquarius, from my twelfth house, was trining Neptune on my eighth cusp; beware two clandestine forces joining together from those positions! The trine just facilitated the ensuing calamity.

There was more. Transiting Uranus was squaring that same Neptune, and transiting Neptune was squaring my eighth house Mercury. Neptune rules drugs and Mercury rules the lungs. They set the scene for one hell of a traumatic evening.

It was a Sunday. It was our beloved Pomeranian Cookie's second birthday and we gave her a party, complete with cake. My parents showed up for the occasion and we had eaten cheesesteaks and fries – not my smartest food choice - while watching a New York Giants football game together.

The heaviness in my stomach gave way to some breathing distress, but I shook it off. My father had done some carpentry repairs in the house, stirring up particles of sawdust which also irritated my breathing. After my parents left for home I headed straight for my nebulizer, primed with albuterol. By then I was really laboring to breathe.

The warning about albuterol was not to overuse it, but nothing was helping. Panic quickly set in. I loaded up the nebulizer for one more shot of it when I felt my chest and back muscles clench as if in a vise grip. There was no more passage of air. My worried partner Janie wanted to take me to the hospital but I couldn't make my way to the car. Janie quickly put in an emergency call to 911.

At that point I thought I might be dying. In my mind's eye I looked for the white light at the end of the tunnel that they say accompanies every death experience. I didn't see anything but pitch black, and as I sank down to the floor I heard the footsteps of six EMT technicians stamping their way into the house, yelling "full respiratory arrest, full arrest!" With no white-lit tunnel in sight, I face-planted on my living room floor and mercifully passed into unconsciousness.

The six EMTs had no time to load me into the ambulance; they had to resuscitate me on the floor of my living room. Poor Janie, who could only sit nearby and watch, recalled that I turned as blue as my jeans. The little blip-blip signals on the telemetry meter came close to flatlining but the EMTs managed to stabilize me. Finally they packed me into the ambulance for the two-block ride to St. Peter's Hospital.

I came to staring up at a bank of greenish fluorescent lights in the same emergency room where I had become such a frequent flyer. There was a sharp stabbing pain in the back of my throat; the supervising physician had been trying without success to intubate me.

"Unbelievable!" I heard him say. "There is no airway – I can't intubate her. Never seen anything like it." I don't know how I resumed breathing if my airway was completely closed off, but that's what I heard him say when I regained consciousness. Everyone registered surprise mixed with immense relief.

Once I became conscious, the EMT techs milled around the gurney, smiling and high-fiving. They deserved an award for snatching me from the brink of death. Beyond the press of the EMT staff stood my worried parents, who had driven all the way back to New Brunswick after Janie alerted them to the emergency. But now everyone was all smiles.

ANYWHERE BUT HERE: CONFESSIONS OF A PISCES MOON

I was in a sorry state on the hospital gurney, drenched in sweat, drained and exhausted, both arms loaded up with IVs, heart racing from the influx of powerful live-saving drugs. During the trauma of the incident I had peed my pants and afterward, vomited all over myself. In spite of the dead seriousness of the situation, I still registered a typically Libran complaint. "Oh, damn! I pissed and puked on my pants. My favorite pants are ruined!"

Still it felt like Christmas. I had survived! I spent the following week in the intensive care unit with both arms strapped to IVs, which made me humbly reliant on my caring nurses for every single thing, especially bedpans. Doctors and nurses kept close monitor on my drug intake and my breathing.

I was finally discharged on Easter Sunday, and the significance of the Resurrection was not lost on me. This absolutely had to be the last massive asthma attack I was ever going to suffer. All the changes I had made for the sake of improvement – the new job, the new house, the move – had only added to the very stress I was supposed to avoid. Time to revisit the drawing board.

It wasn't scary enough that I had almost died on the floor of my living room. Even more devastating was that I had almost died having accomplished nothing of value in my life. That realization had a profoundly disturbing effect that resonated within me for many months, and perhaps years, afterward. Having spared me, the Grim Reaper delivered a grim message: now go and make something of yourself.

Those with heavy eighth house or Scorpionic placements often undergo major transformations or rebuilds in response to life crises. With four planets in my eighth such was the case with me. We are accustomed to rebuilds, but we must design them well, or the structures collapse and the whole cycle begins again.

This time I absolutely had to get it right. I felt I had achieved nothing and somehow I now had to make my life matter; I had to begin making something of myself, making some kind of contribution. At long last, finally a goal, however still amorphous at the time, began to form.

My job change had taken me out of the City to a much slower-paced New Jersey corporation that was only a half hour by car from my home. Leaving the long commute and the frantic Manhattan rat race behind seemed to be a step in the right direction.

But the new job did not offer the solution I was seeking, and it became another source of dissatisfaction. What was I going to do now, what direction would I take? I had neglected my metaphysical studies for some years, leaving a large void in my life that now demanded attention. But someone was going to toss me a lifeline.

In the spring of 1994 I received a phone call from my old astrologer buddy; Lee Lehman was coming to New York for a conference and wanted to meet up. We met for lunch at a café inside the newly renovated Grand Central Station, which had been wonderfully restored to its original majestic stature.

Lee and I caught up on life events and accomplishments, mostly hers. Since our last meeting she had experienced a meteoric rise in the field of astrology, having taught numerous classes, lectured around the world, and published several books. I, on the other hand, was still drifting listlessly through space.

Lee spoke about her plans to teach a course in horary astrology, something that I had not heard of. Horary, meaning "hour," is a branch of astrology that answers questions based on a chart cast for the time that the question is understood by the astrologer.

I was intrigued – you can really answer questions with astrology? Of course you can. Lee happened to have with her a copy of William

ANYWHERE BUT HERE: CONFESSIONS OF A PISCES MOON

Lilly's huge Seventeenth Century opus, *Christian Astrology,* which I purchased from her on the spot. I was about to make the acquaintance of the master of horary astrology. Windows to the sky were opening again.

In keeping with my new passion I began reading books by other classical masters of astrology - Bonatti, Masha'allah, and Ptolemy, while adding modern ones like Ivy Goldstein-Jacobson, Anthony Louis, and Barbara Watters. My library kept pace with my enthusiasm for this new knowledge.

I owe Ms. Watters a huge debt of gratitude; in the Sixties she published an obscure but ground-breaking book entitled *The Astrologer Looks At Murder.* As a true crime fan I was fascinated to see that astrology, specifically, event charts, could also be employed to gain information about crimes. For once my disparate interests – astrology, the occult, and true crime - were beginning to coalesce.

The lifeline Lee had thrown me started an entirely new cycle of astrological research. I was still dogged by the fact that I still hadn't accomplished anything of value in my life. My paralegal career, now covering an incredible span of almost twenty years – that career that I had been trying to leave for so long - had offered stability, a good livelihood, and steady employment, but at the cost of constantly having to reinvent my commitment to it.

Finally the do-or-die moment arrived. Massage therapy had not provided the escape hatch to self-employment that I had been seeking, so I moved further up the alternative health chain. When I was ill I received several treatments of acupuncture to help alleviate my asthmatic condition, and they had proven invaluable. I wanted to learn more about energy, which is what acupuncture basically entails. The choice lie clearly ahead of me: I was going to study acupuncture.

An acupuncture school previously located in Connecticut had just relocated to the Chelsea district of Manhattan. It was a sign. I applied to attend the school, and in September 1995 enrolled at the Tri-State College of Acupuncture for a three-year intensive course leading to board certification, licensure, and the degree of Diplomate of Acupuncture (Dipl. Ac. or L.Ac.)

In my quest to feel some sense of accomplishment I had charted a very ambitious course. It was one that could prove extremely rewarding, if I could only avoid the curse of Jupiter rising: overdoing it to the point of severe burnout. Something I was well familiar with by then.

Now, instead of passing out at the sight of a needle, I was going to be handling them and placing them into patients! It was a paradigm shift of momentous proportions for me. And I was miraculously able to do that with minimal anxiety. Sea changes had indeed taken place!

Here I need to address two things that have always bothered me about the public perception of acupuncture. Acupuncture contains two words that I believe were deliberately selected to instill fear and apprehension in people. First, "puncture" is a horrible word to insert into the name of any healing therapy; it conjures up the frightening image of circular holes in one's skin not unlike gunshot wounds. There is no "puncturing" of the individual during an acupuncture treatment; in fact, acupuncture needles are so delicate that they can be bent in half with the twist of a finger. They are nothing like the regular needles used for injections or blood draws. I have always objected to the word "acupuncture," which automatically instills fear into people. Words have a power all their own.

The second objection on my list is the term "needles". Acupuncture needles are slight, delicate filaments barely thicker than a human hair that are tapped into the surface of the skin. There is a much fear of acupuncture among the public because of the image conveyed by the

ANYWHERE BUT HERE: CONFESSIONS OF A PISCES MOON

word "puncture" and the mention of needles, which many people dread. For that reason I have always referred to them as "filaments" rather than needles.

That being said, people had already undergone a fair amount of indoctrination against "acupuncture needles" and my clients' fear of the needles was a constant issue in my practice. If anything, there is a sensation of a pinch, and sometimes more in a sensitive spot, but the effect is quick while the results can be long lasting. So much for my defense of a much maligned and little understood alternative therapy that I have witnessed to work wonders time and again, especially on myself.

It's funny to think that all of my career pursuits – astrology, acupuncture, occult symbolism, and conspiracy theory – have been scoffed at, mocked, and criticized by skeptics, but being an Aquarius rising, these attacks on my credibility have only strengthened my inner reserve to continue on my path. Aquarians will go their own way regardless of peer pressure.

In my birth chart Mars appears in the tenth house of career in Sagittarius, and one can imagine the needles as little arrows! Mars forms a conjunction with Chiron and a tight trine to sixth house Pluto in Leo, attesting to my abilities with healing energies.

I called upon this healing power when I was sick with the Epstein-Barr virus, and at that time acupuncture had been extremely effective in helping me regain my health. On a sleazier note, the Mars-Pluto aspect was also activated during all the bizarre sexual encounters I faced during my European trip with Gigi. Mars-Pluto has proven to be a potent aspect with many faces, some more salacious than others.

During the first month of my acupuncture training Uranus and Neptune were both journeying through the sign of Capricorn, touching off square aspects to my Libra planets from the twelfth house to the eighth, probably not the best departure point for a new venture. Jupiter was in the sign of Sagittarius, nearing my Midheaven – a career with sharp objects resembling arrows!

I loved my acupuncture training. It taught me a great deal about healing and alternative technologies that I still use to this day. At graduation in 1998 I received my diploma from Tri-State College of Acupuncture in New York, an excellent school that is unfortunately no longer in existence. That graduation day ranks high on the list as one of the best days of my life. It was an accomplishment. I was beginning to feel that all was not lost.

While my acupuncture training was intensely rewarding, it took a toll on me mentally and physically. I had to juggle three part-time jobs while attending classes on one weeknight, several weekdays, and most weekends. Once again I was managing many diverse responsibilities at once.

My near-death experience had prodded me to make something of my life, yet here I was dancing with the same demons that had threatened my health in the past. I was feeling run down, drained, and lethargic, warning symptoms for a former Epstein-Barr sufferer. Something serious was about to give. But this time I heeded the warning in a very unusual and unexpected way.

My daily one-hour train commute to New York was one of the healthier aspects of my work and school experience. It allowed me time to relax, study, or listen to lectures on my Walkman. It was the only time I had to decompress after long days at school and work. Inspirational lectures by Deepak Chopra, Gregg Braden, and Caroline Myss energized my spirits. It was a Caroline Myss lecture one evening that shot me bolt upright in my seat: Urgent action required!

ANYWHERE BUT HERE: CONFESSIONS OF A PISCES MOON

It was early November 1997. I had just taken and passed my acupuncture board exams for national certification. I was reeling from exhaustion and feeling anxious about relapsing. The cassette in my Walkman was a talk by Caroline Myss on spiritual fulfillment. This particular message struck a bullseye in my consciousness. Her lecture went something like this:

"If you are not feeling connected in spirit to your work, you owe it to yourself to leave it! Staying stuck in an unfulfilling position will sap your energies and drain you (something I had experienced time and again). If you aren't happy at what you are doing, you are only delaying, and denying, your spiritual growth, and there may be unwanted consequences." (something else I had also experienced).

That message stuck in my craw. She's so right, I thought. How many times do I have to reinvent and recreate myself just to get myself into the office every day and perform tasks that I don't give a damn about? Enough is enough!

I didn't give the message a second thought. As if on autopilot I breezed into work the next morning and immediately gave two weeks' notice of quitting. It was a bold move, one that would not truck any willy-nilly Libran or Piscean waffling. I didn't worry about how I was going to pay my mortgage, manage the household bills, or how I would afford anything at all. I just quit.

And it felt wonderful. I wanted to save my spirit, and I knew Spirit would come through for me. And She did, in a most miraculous way.

I left the job the week of Thanksgiving, feeling more reason than ever to be grateful and happy for such guidance. I didn't worry about the money; I trusted Spirit to keep me afloat. I didn't always have such trust in the Universe, and sadly admit that sometimes I still don't now, but it's something I still work at.

B D SALERNO

It is said that all Piscean Suns and Moons are addicted to something; my vice of preference is casino gambling. During my more affluent years I would take occasional trips to the Atlantic City casinos for a day of excitement. Cards had always held a fascination for me and I developed a fondness for video poker. Every year when I had time off around Christmas I would make a special gambling trip to AC.

I really couldn't afford to gamble, but my instinct was strong and I followed it. I was able to muster up only around $40 for the trip, which is next to nothing for an afternoon of even the most frugal gambling, but I was feeling inspired.

As I entered the casino I cashed in a free play voucher for $15. Near the cashier's cage was a bank of video Joker Poker machines featuring a progressive jackpot of $3,150 for the first player who got five of a kind.

I inserted the voucher into the machine and played two hands. On the third hand I was dealt three tens (my birth month is October), and the deal awarded me the fourth ten and the joker – five tens! Within the first ten minutes I had won the $3,150 progressive jackpot!

Spirit was right to send me to the casino! I had a very profitable day, bringing home the original $3,150 plus a little more.

The planetary transits helped set me up for a lucky day: Venus squared my Sun from the twelfth to the eighth houses. Not all squares give problems, as my Venus and Sun are conjoined natally. Mars squared Venus from the eleventh to the eighth. That was a good aspect as well, as they sextile natally. From my eleventh house of goals and dreams Jupiter in Aquarius trined eight house Neptune on the eighth house cusp of other people's money.

That windfall was enough to get me through the final semester of acupuncture school without having to work. My only other commitment was to give two massages a week for two clients who paid well. I finally had time to finish my studies without the stress and pressure of juggling three jobs. It was miraculous. Caroline Myss' advice had stood me in good stead, as had my intuition, guided by Spirit. Sometimes it pays to take that blind leap of faith.

Unfortunately, school landed me in such deep debt that it was a struggle to make a living afterward. The aspects facing me upon graduation were financially challenging as well. Transiting Saturn was slowly grinding out an opposition to my eighth house Libra stellium, causing all manner of delays and obstacles to gaining steady employment and income, as well as the financial hardship brought on by the student loan. The AIDS epidemic had made medical professionals extremely wary of needles, and that fear cost me two promised full-time positions in doctors' offices before the jobs even started.

As with my massage therapy career, I had to set out on my own, no small feat for someone with no contacts, no established reputation, and no prospective clientele.

In addition to the harsh Saturn transits, Jupiter was also opposing natal Saturn, putting a crimp on any opportunities. It was not an auspicious time to set out in a new profession. I got various jobs practicing in a few clinics whose sole function was to gouge the insurance companies of monies paid out by no-fault accident insurance. I loved my work but it was an unsavory way to make a living. One doctor I worked for ended up in prison for insurance fraud, another was sanctioned by the state medical board, while many others went on illegally padding their wallets undetected.

It became impossible to meet the burden of debt and still pay my regular bills. I was blessed that one of my former employers hired me back to do paralegal work; I really needed the money and could not hold out for an offer to practice acupuncture. My proposed career in alternative health fell by the wayside within a few short years. But by then I was actively practicing astrology again, and I was about to cast the most important chart of my lifetime.

CHAPTER FIFTEEN

THE 21st CENTURY

The early 2000s proved decidedly Uranian: I was heavily involved in crime, or forensic, astrology and the work inspired me to delve deeply into the classical astrology of the ancients. My purchase of the William Lilly book from Lee had started the process, and when acupuncture school ended in 1998 I once again revisited the arcane art.

Yet something was missing – a solid reference text with samples to illustrate just how a crime chart should be read. The ancients spoke at great length about thefts and various misdeeds, but gave few concrete examples. One exception was a famous example given by William Lilly in *Christian Astrology* – a description of how he used an astrology chart to solve the theft of fish and vegetables from his home. Using astrological principles he identified the thief and actually recovered some of the stolen food. But most of the ancient texts did not offer example charts, and as I studied, a seed became planted in my mind for future cultivation.

At the time my partner Janie, who was studying history at Rutgers, was researching the notorious kidnapping of Charles Lindbergh Jr. in 1932. We discussed the case at length and I read up on it, anxious to try my hand at what would be my first crime chart.

The results were remarkable; applying the technique described in Barbara Watter's 1964 book *The Astrologer Looks At Murder* I was able to discern many of the facts of the kidnapping just from reviewing the planetary signs and positions. This was the catalyst to casting many more crime charts based on incidents in the news, and I was well on my way to learning what we now call "forensic astrology". Little did I know then that my article on the Lindbergh case would eventually become the first chapter of my first book some ten years later, entitled *Forensics by the Stars: Astrology Investigates*.

In 2002 the four outer giants, Saturn, Neptune, Pluto, and especially Uranus, conspired to reshape my destiny. My attempts at establishing an acupuncture practice had driven me into even deeper debt than when I left school. I had clung to temporary paralegal work to make ends meet, but still longed for some form of livelihood that I could create and call my own. Enter the internet, ruled by my Ascendant co-ruler, and ruler of cyberspace, Uranus.

For a large portion of that year Uranus was in trine aspect to my Libra stellium, which lies between 17 and 27 degrees of Libra. Neptune had just entered Uranus' sign, Aquarius, and Pluto, at my Midheaven, was approaching conjunction with tenth house Mars. Mars rules my money second house; this new internet enterprise was about to earn me more money than I ever thought possible in a home-based business. Finally my prayers for self-employment were answered in earnest. The outer giants were offering exciting new opportunities and I was quick to jump on the internet bandwagon.

Guided by sheer serendipity and chance encounters with several people I discovered a unique health product from Asia that assisted the body's detoxification process. The product consisted of pouches containing various minerals and herbs that, when applied to the soles of the feet, or any soft area of the body, would draw out toxic substances.

This product often drew the criticism of uninformed skeptics, but that was nothing new to me. The product it also helped countless others resolve a number of physical complaints - mostly the latter. The foot patches drew rave reviews for helping people relax, sleep better, lose weight, and resolve stubborn skin disorders. I sold the patches to some seriously ill people who became regular customers and swore by the product. They had lost all faith in the medical profession and claimed that only the detoxification patches were keeping them going.

It was what I had always hoped to hear about acupuncture, but I gladly accepted the trade-off. It was extremely rewarding to know that I was helping people. They also reported overall improvements in their health just because the patches had such a calming effect. I was quickly sold on the product's value, and in 2003 I began importing it from Japan.

Within months I was matching my paralegal income and then some. I created my own website, then a second site, and began to learn HTML, online marketing, SEO, and web marketing. The internet was still in its infancy in terms of marketing potential and the social media were still in gestation stage, with MySpace the only platform. The challenge of creating web content lifted my generally left-brained, dry legalese to writing innovative, creative blurbs and paragraphs to promote my product. Writing was becoming fun again.

As much as I felt disconnected from my paralegal work, it came in very handy when I had to deal with documents and clients. I was still working with foreign businesses but in an entirely different medium. My seemingly disjointed career experiences were beginning to blend together nicely in this new venture.

By 2006 I was earning six figures from the internet alone, and took the gargantuan risk of taking early retirement from my job. Pluto crossing my Mars had awarded me handsomely money-wise; it was hard to believe how I had shot from nearly $50K in school-related debt to a six-figure income just within the span of a seven-year Saturn cycle. It also helped that I sold my first house in New Brunswick for a nice profit and bought another house in a nearby town away from the chaos of the Rutgers campus.

But what had I said about Jupiterian overconfidence? It was a wild ride, but like all good things, all nice transits must come to an end, and mine did in the iconic crash year of 2008. It was an unjolly Jupiter to herald the time of reckoning.

I am blessed to have the protection of benevolent Jupiter on my Ascendant, but I'm the first to point out that there's an unfavorable side to the Jovian giant that can bring one to the brink of ruin. Overconfidence can lead to bad judgment and unrealistic thinking – remember that Jupiter also rules Pisces, not the strongest suit in the business-minded logic department.

In 2008 along came transiting Jupiter in stern Capricorn, its unhappy sign of fall, to square all my Libran planets. With Capricorn ruling business, all the rookie mistakes I made – not setting aside enough money, investing in new products without sufficient market research, splurging on a vacation condo in Arizona, and just plain blowing money on whatever I wanted – came back to bite me like a rabid dog.

Neptune also formed a trine to my Mercury/Venus combo, adding confused thinking to the mix where there was already an abundance of it. To top it off, the Moon's North Node, a deceptive placement, was right on said Jupiter and my Ascendant. I wasn't seeing the warning signs of a looming business crash until they t-boned me at mach speed.

Things unraveled quickly, aided by some very nefarious moves by Google, who saw fit to shuffle SEO rankings for no apparently good reason. My solid number one SEO rankings for my site dropped overnight to Google's page 5, no man's land. Sales dropped literally overnight, then vanished. Try as I did to positive-think my way through the crisis, my prospects were bleak.

By end of 2008 I had to blow up my credit cards in order to stay afloat, and just two years into what I imagined would be a comfy early retirement I was deeply in debt and in search of a job. The sting of this failure paralyzed me for a few fitful months of self-recrimination and blame until an ad on Craigslist caught my attention.

"WANTED: Acupuncturist with NJ State license for full-time work in chiropractic clinic. Salary $75,000/year." I never picked up a phone so fast. And I never heaved a sigh of relief so intensely. By the end of that week I was reporting to a clinic as staff acupuncturist. Saved again by the celestial bell, just in time for my second go-round with Saturn's stern 28-year cycle. An unexpected change of was coming that had nothing to do with acupuncture and everything to do with writing a book.

The clinic was open from 9 AM until 7 PM, a long day broken up by a three-hour lunch break. The job was a forty-minute drive from home, too far to go home for lunch, so I would have to find some other way to spend the time.

Suburban New Jersey towns do not have much to offer in the way of entertainment, but my dilemma was quickly resolved: I decided to spend my lunch breaks studying forensic astrology and working on crime charts. With my internet business now a vague memory, I once again had time for my astrology work. And my internet experience had exposed me to blogging, a natural outlet for all kinds of writing.

I joined a true crime astrology blog where I came across a community of astrologers who were also writing about crime astrology. Day after day, during lunch hours, I scanned the news for crime stories, cast the charts, wrote them up and posted the articles in the blog. I didn't know it then, but important seeds were being planted regarding my future. My desire to create something worthwhile, to make some kind of contribution for someone somewhere, was about to take root.

Soon I had amassed some forty articles on murdered and missing persons, thanks to those long lunch hour breaks. Then came a fateful conversation with Angela Dumas, a classmate from acupuncture school who has been a dear friend ever since.

"You have like thirty, forty articles on crime astrology? You should just write a book!" she exclaimed. Writing a book felt like a daunting task, even if I published it myself. The idea of it stirred both excitement and apprehension.

"But I'm not an expert astrologer. I don't have the credentials to publish this type of work. I just started using some techniques and they work, that's all." In reality I was fearing criticism and blowback from my peers, all of whom seemed so much better schooled in astrology than I.

After all, they had been practicing and refining their skills while I was slow dancing in and out of astrology for several years. But after much self-deprecating nonsense I gave Angela's suggestion some serious thought.

It was time. People needed to know that astrology could be used to solve crimes. It was time for me to put up or shut up. A book on crime astrology could provide the impetus for others to take up the craft and develop it even further. Maybe law enforcement would take notice; if police turned to psychics at a last resort why couldn't they also consult astrologers?

The idea of a book struck an old chord in me. As a child and teenager I was a prolific writer and many fellow classmates from my high school remembered me that way. In my mind writing a book was a weighty accomplishment. True, that was in times long past when books were only published by publishing houses who routinely rejected most of their submissions. As a novice with no agent or previous experience I felt I wouldn't stand a chance at securing a publishing deal.

ANYWHERE BUT HERE: CONFESSIONS OF A PISCES MOON

But books still meant the world to me. A book about an obscure branch of astrology would be a contribution to my fellow astrologers as well as up-and-coming students who were interested in the techniques. I didn't have to be an expert - I still do not consider myself an expert now. I just had to explain the techniques I was using and show how they actually worked. Others would hopefully become inspired and take the work to yet another level. Here and now, in 2024, I am glad to note that many other excellent astrologers have done just that and made their work accessible on Youtube, Instagram, and other wide-reaching platforms.

Angela had coined a funny nickname for me during our three years of school together – "Barbie Doll," a spin on my birth name, Barbara (though I prefer to be called either Barb or B.D.). It was a term of endearment, but also hysterical, because I, an introverted nerd, am the antithesis of anything remotely Barbie Doll-like.

The cute nickname stuck, and in time Barbie Doll became "B.D." and B.D. became me. When I finally decided, after much wringing of hands and gnashing of teeth, to put all my astrology work into a book, Angela was among the first to cheer me on.

"If I succeed in actually completing this book, and I'm not sure I will, but if I do, I will write under the pen name B.D. Salerno in your honor," I promised her. And so it went. I found a self-publisher who gave birth to my first book, *Forensics by the Stars: Astrology Investigates*, on October 25, 2012, just days after my own birthday. A Scorpio book about using astrology in crime analysis – what a perfect Sun sign!

Naturally, Jupiter, ruler of my tenth house, was then transiting Gemini, sign of books and writers. A whole new career was born, but not without Saturn's influence. The ringed giant was bearing down on my Libra stellium, exerting pressure on my final work product, with endless editing, revising, second-guessing, taking work out, adding work in.

The grim taskmaster was having his say, testing my confidence in my work and myself to the limit. I kept my goal afloat only by constantly visualizing the finished paperback in my hands. And by applying the power of prayer to my work – more on that later.

I often tricked myself by thinking that the book was nearly done, which softened the harsh reality that it would take at least another six months to a year to be done to my satisfaction. That way the finish line always felt within reach. Self-deception comes naturally to the Piscean Moon native. It's not always a bad thing when it's for a good cause.

Once the book was out I wanted to write more. I had begun in-depth studies of the ancient astrologers and wanted to test out the advice they offered regarding the human condition. Such texts were not available until the early 1990s when a wonderful effort made by several prominent astrologers, called Project Hindsight, resulted in the translation and publication of many arcane astrological texts. These texts were gold mines of information about human frailties and misadventures. I was already preparing a second, much more comprehensive work that put the ancient aphorisms to the test. To make the work interesting to the readers I chose celebrity crimes to promote the ancient teachings.

My second book presented the same challenges as the first – was I competent to put the ancient masters to the test, what if I made mistakes, what if my explanations were not sufficient to make my point? Such are the issues that result from an excessive overthinker like myself, with six placements in air signs.

My second book, *Exploring Forensic Astrology: The Secrets Behind Famous Family Murders,* issued in June 2016. It was an incredibly active time astrologically. Saturn had been slowly passing across my Midheaven, appropriate because I had retired just months earlier, and it promised rewards after so much hard work.

ANYWHERE BUT HERE: CONFESSIONS OF A PISCES MOON

Venus, passing through the writer's sign Gemini, briefly made an opposition to Saturn, while Mars in Scorpio moved through my ninth house of publishing – in Scorpio, the sign of true crime, no less. Venus rules my third of books and writing and Uranus rules astrology!

Neptune was sitting on my Moon for an added splash of dreamy Piscean energy, so ethereal that I have no idea what even happened there. Pluto in Capricorn was beginning to square my Libran planets, beginning with Neptune, so I was in for a transformative ride.

I faced some stiff challenges to usher in the twenty-teens. The most difficult challenge by far of my lifetime was not my horrendous car accident, my health problems, or even my near-death adventure; it was providing care for my parents, who were in their nineties and suffering from dementia. I had always planned on taking care of them when the time came, but I was not prepared for the extreme mental and emotional stress that it exacted. My sister had moved from Virginia Beach into my home to tend to their needs while I was still working. Eventually it was necessary to also move my parents into my home as they could no longer fend for themselves.

It was an emotionally draining time. The research and writing of my books gave me some respite from the sadness and frustration of watching my parents' slow decline into dementia, and sometimes, madness. As a child writing had given me a welcome escape from tensions in the home, and the same proved true even now. After I lost my father in 2014 writing also gave me a daily discipline to adhere to while I struggled through a myriad of difficult emotions.

After my mother passed away in 2018 I felt a huge void – what next? My parents were gone, my second book was done, I had just retired from my job, and I was at loose ends - but not for long. There was one crime that had always stuck in my memory and I decided to look further into it.

Thus was born my next venture, which brought me places I never expected to go. What had I said about Pluto in Capricorn squaring my Libran Sun? It had to do with a true crime investigation – something I had never before attempted, but something that would completely commandeer my life for the next three years.

I was fifteen years old in July 1966 when eight Chicago student nurses were brutally murdered in their dormitory townhouse. As a sensitive teen just a few years younger than the nurses I was completely horrified by the crime. It was the one crime that I, as a true crime aficionado, could never quite get out of my head. I decided to take a look at that crime chart and see if there was a blog article or chapter of a new book hidden within the story. I had no idea what I was getting myself into.

Something about the crime chart was off. It couldn't have happened at 11:00 PM as the sole surviving witness, a nurse who had escaped murder by hiding under a bed, had recounted. But there were other things wrong as well. The crime narrative, of one drunken, drugged-out man overpowering nine healthy, strong young nurses, was suspicious.

Before I knew it I had launched into the beginning of a three-year investigation into the crime, which resulted in my third book, *Richard Speck and the Eight Nurses: Deconstructing A Mass Murder.* This was a total departure from any type of work I had ever done. I'm not an investigator, an attorney, a detective, or a journalist. I just dug into every bit of information I could get my hands on. I filed FOIA requests with the Chicago Police Department, the FBI, and the Coast Guard; I ordered autopsy reports from the Chicago Medical Examiner's Office, and I read every book, article, and watched every video I could find.

It was a mammoth effort. I was often overwhelmed by it, feeling inadequate for the task at hand and ignorant of how to organize and present it in a cohesive piece of work. The major impact of the book is that it reveals facts and evidence never previously written about

ANYWHERE BUT HERE: CONFESSIONS OF A PISCES MOON

that cast a whole different light on the crime. Through my research I uncovered vital information never before revealed. In my opinion, the murders involved massive deception, a diabolical cover-up, and a huge miscarriage of justice.

The book both intimidated me and challenged me during those three years. I credit the power of prayer with helping me stay the course. It is a regular habit that for me to pray before writing. I always thank God, my guardian angels, and my personal muses, for helping with my projects. It helps me set my intent and my focus. It helps me navigate through the awkward morass of self-doubt and insecurity that many writers like myself struggle with during the creation of a written work.

Quick on the heels of *Deconstructing* I assembled a fourth book to expose and explain all the occult references and symbols that I came across in my research. This gave rise to the fastest book I ever wrote – *Desperate Rites: Astrology and the Occult in the Richard Speck Murders,* which issued in October 2023, just months after the release of *Deconstructing.* Now, in addition to crime astrology, I analyze and explain the occult side of crimes as shown in the imagery, numerology, and symbolism that is ever present, yet goes unnoticed by the general public.

True crime is a strange obsession: you invest your time and energy in studying horrific events, yet all the while wishing that they never happened. Yet you still engage them and feel compelled to make sense of them, and even solve them. I am compelled to carry out my eighth house destiny of occult investigations, but I also wish that none of those awful things ever happened. My Pisces Moon, in spite of everything, still yearns to be somewhere else – anywhere but here – to "go home" to those elusive celestial bodies. Someday that yearning will be fulfilled, but for now, there I have many more contributions to make.

More books are in the pipeline. I am planning to make *Desperate Rites* into a series of books that will delve into the more nefarious aspects of true crime, like Satanism, false flags, MK Ultra mind control, massive political corruption, and the like.

Saturn is now transiting my first house in Pisces, so I am giving very serious thought to my next projects, and Uranus is transiting my third, giving me flashes of intuition as to how to go about them. Uranus in the third also gave me the impetus to write this book - the planetary ruler of astrology transiting the third house of communication, thought, and writing – perfect timing!

I am eternally grateful for that scary night in April 1992 when I was granted the miracle of a second chance to fulfill my life path. I hope that my works will have made that meaningful contribution that I felt was missing from my life - for astrologers, true crime addicts like myself, and for anyone who wants to seek guidance from the stars.

After decades of all the distraction-filled drama, I think I've finally found that elusive purpose - to study what I love and share it with others. I will keep doing that until I can't anymore. At some future point I will finally return "home" to swing on a star, but there's no rush. If I have learned anything else, it's that "here" is not such a bad place after all.

CONTACT INFORMATION

Twitter/X: @starsleuth

Instagram: bdsalerno21

Telegram/Skype: B.D. Salerno

Youtube channels: Starsleuth, ReverseWorld

Website: http://www.strangebuttruecrime.com

Books:

Forensics by the Stars: Astrology Investigates (2012)

Exploring Forensic Astrology: The Secrets Behind Famous Family Murders (2016)

Richard Speck and the Eight Nurses: Deconstructing A Mass Murder (2023)

Desperate Rites, vol I: Astrology and the Occult in the Richard Speck Murders (2023)

Anywhere But Here: Confessions of a Pisces Moon (2024)

Asteroids, Our Cosmic Influencers (2025)

Desperate Rites, vol II: Astrology and the Occult in the Black Dahlia Murder (2025)

Don't miss out!

Visit the website below and you can sign up to receive emails whenever B D SALERNO publishes a new book. There's no charge and no obligation.

https://books2read.com/r/B-A-WFDW-ZBJTC

BOOKS2READ

Connecting independent readers to independent writers.

Did you love *Anywhere But Here: Confessions of A Pisces Moon*? Then you should read *Asteroids Our Cosmic Influencers*[1] by B D SALERNO!

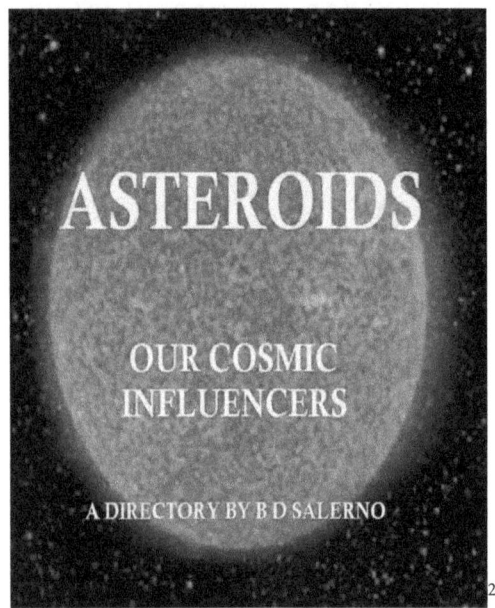

A directory of over 400 asteroids, centaurs, TNOs and other minor planets, including their numbers, discovery data, backstories and mythological connections, with astrological interpretations and examples of their influence in the horoscopes of well-known individuals.

---

1. https://books2read.com/u/mqOpMe

2. https://books2read.com/u/mqOpMe

Also by B D SALERNO

Desperate Rites
Desperate Rites: Astrology and the Occult in the Richard Speck Murders

Standalone
Richard Speck and the Eight Nurses: Deconstructing A Mass Murder
Richard Speck and the Eight Nurses: Deconstructing A Mass Murder
Anywhere But Here: Confessions of A Pisces Moon
Asteroids Our Cosmic Influencers

About the Author

BD Salerno attended Rutgers University in New Jersey and also obtained professional secondary education in New York City. Her eclectic interests include alternative healing, true crime, music, and astrology.

www.ingramcontent.com/pod-product-compliance
Lightning Source LLC
LaVergne TN
LVHW091309080426
835510LV00007B/437